THE PRICE OF HONESTY

life, laughter and liquid lunches

RALPH COSTELLO

Brunswick Press

Edited by Barry Norris.
Cover photos courtesy of Frances Costello.
Cover and book design by Jaye Haworth.
Art direction by Julie Scriver.
Printed in Canada.
10 9 8 7 6 5 4 3 2 1

Library and Archives Canada Cataloguing in Publication

Costello, Ralph
The price of honesty: life, laughter and liquid lunches / Ralph Costello.

ISBN 978-0-88790-200-0

1. Saint John (N.B.)—Anecdotes. 2. Saint John (N.B.)—Biography.
3. Saint John (N.B.)—History. 4. Costello, Ralph—Anecdotes. I. Title.

FC2497.4.C68 2011   971.5'32   C2011-907210-6

ISBN 978-0-88790-200-0

Brunswick News Inc. would like to acknowledge the kind support of Frances Costello and Peter McGuire, who supplied the photographs that appear on the cover and pages 149 to 156; David Spragg, who performed archival research and prepared the photographs for publication; and Fred Hazel, who was instrumental in seeing this manuscript through from idea to the final proofs.

Brunswick Press
c/o Brunswick News Inc.
210 Crown St.
Saint John, NB E2L 3V8

To Readers Who Enjoy a Good Story

Contents

SOME GOOD BOOKS 215

A TOUCH OF WHIMSY 239

THE SPOKEN WORD 267

INTRODUCTION

– – – – – – –
– – – – –
–

RALPH COSTELLO was a gifted storyteller. He made his living telling people's stories as a reporter, editor, and publisher of two great New Brunswick newspapers, the *Evening Times-Globe* and the *Telegraph-Journal*.

He was exceptionally good at the business of observing people, picking up and interpreting their ideas and emotions. But his skills ran deeper than that. He loved the craft of writing. Readers can feel that in this collection of some of the personal pieces he wrote over the years.

He managed to do quite a few other things as well — starting out as a part-time sports writer with the two newspapers. He eventually became publisher of these newspapers, and president of the Canadian Daily Newspapers' Association, of the Canadian Press, and of the Royal Canadian Golf Association.

But writing remained his first love. He was one of those self-taught people, in the days before schools of journalism. His craft was the use of words to tell a story, to present a picture that would engage readers. His aim — which he tried to impress on the writers under his direction — was to "make your stories sing — take the readers there with you."

In this collection, readers will see just how well Ralph Costello was able to do those things himself. Some of these stories — and that's what he always called them—have been published before in the newspapers; many appear in this volume for the first time.

Read them with an eye for the enthusiasm, the love, and the magic he put into them. You'll encounter stories of humble beginnings, of youthful yearnings, of universal ideals, glimpses of the grandeur and the glitter of important people, and the simple aspirations of ordinary people.

There's a great deal of humour, pathos, sentiment, and wise understanding of the human condition in this writing. You can hear these stories sing in the short, snappy sentences, the authentic dialogue, the crisp ideas, and the profound understanding of the life people are wrapped up in. And a lot of warm, human emotion.

As an old-school newspaper publisher, Ralph Costello often had to play the tough-guy role. Reading these stories, you'll find out who my old friend and mentor really was.

—Fred Hazel

PROLOGUE

"ASIDE FROM THAT, Mrs. Lincoln, how did you enjoy the play?"

That classic, albeit cynical, post-historical quip has a lot to say about life.

I'm not at all sure what Mary Todd Lincoln's reply would have been if she had been asked that question the night of April 14, 1865, which happened to fall on Good Friday. That was the night her husband, Abraham Lincoln, 16th president of the United States, was shot to death by John Wilkes Booth while attending a play at Ford's Theatre in Washington, D.C.

How do any of us enjoy the brief time on the stage that has been our life?

Speaking for myself, I've enjoyed the play very much, virtually every minute of it. I have been writing all my life, and I write now from the perspective of an ending — or a new beginning — in sight.

I can look back at the lifetime view of a young boy from The Other Side Of The Tracks, a child of the Great Depression, a newsboy who became a newspaper publisher and president of a couple of national news organizations, an aspiring caddie who went on to become president of the Royal Canadian Golf Association, the Canadian Golf Foundation, and the Canadian Golf Hall of Fame.

I don't propose to brag, because modesty has been part of my makeup. But ambition — and I guess hard work — took me to the presidency of the Canadian

Daily Newspaper Publishers' Association and of the Canadian Press. It was the people I met along this journey who made it interesting and exciting.

I've enjoyed it all. Life became good to me. I was lucky, maybe the right person at the right time, or maybe even the wrong person at the right time.

For me, it was a time of challenge and we learned to live with adversity. We learned to be optimistic in an era when there was no apparent reason for optimism. We learned to be competitive to survive, competitive in sport, and competitive in business.

Was the Depression of my youth depressing? Of course. You can read here about a family fearing a knock on the door—only to realize it was a church group with presents from the Christmas Empty Stocking Fund that operated in our community.

I can share stories about the long, eternal wait for the father coming home on payday, the man with the weakness—would he come home, would he have any money left? And the heartbreak of turning a deaf ear to friends who pounded on the door for a friendly visit when there was no way to offer them a cup of tea.

There have been lean years and good years. I've encountered a lot of interesting people. Like many of you, I've had an interesting family, a good family life, and from the whole experience, I think there are a few good stories to tell. Enjoy them.

Yes, I enjoyed the play.

—Ralph Costello

EDITOR'S NOTE

— —— —— —— —
—— —— —
—

DURING THE AMERICAN CIVIL WAR, journalists reporting from the field filed their stories to newspapers using railroad telegraph offices. It was customary for telegraphers to end a transmission by typing "**XXX**." Since these three letters do not appear side by side in any English word, **XXX** signaled clearly that the transmission was over.

"**XXX**" is also the Roman numeral for "30." As the telegraph era of reporting gave way to wire services and electronic typesetting, the designation "30" continued to be used by reporters, editors and linotype operators to signal that the last word had been written. It is still used today to end many stories and press releases.

As a longtime reporter and editor, Ralph Costello ended each chapter of these columns and memoirs with -30-, and we've preserved that convention. These are his last words and final dispatch to the public — the summation of his life in sport and journalism.

-30-

CORRIDORS OF POWER

Beaverbrook's Love for New Brunswick
Manifest Everywhere

— — — — — — —
— — — — —
—

CHIEF JOHN SIMON of the Big Cove Reserve was there, and so was Chief Mosey Francis of the Eel Ground Reserve, and Chief Raymond Tremblay of the Tobique Reserve, and Oliver Polchies of the Woodstock Reserve.

They had been flown to London from New Brunswick to add colour to the spectacular ceremonies that would honour one of New Brunswick's favourite sons.

Oil billionaire J. Paul Getty was among those present.

And so were Lord Morrison of Lambeth, Sir Christopher Chancellor, The Earl of Rosebery, Lord Normanbrook, Sir Isaac Wilson, Viscount Rothermere, and many other great figures of the time.

K.C. Irving, Dr. Colin B. Mackay, Brigadier Michael Wardell, and J.K. Grainger were there from New Brunswick.

The guard of honour was made up of members of the Royal Canadian Mounted Police, and Royal Air Force Trumpeters were there from the band of the Royal Air Force College at Cranwell.

The program of music was played by The Maple Leaf Six and included "Pomp and Circumstance," "Alouette," "Home On The Range," and "The Whiffenpoof Song," selections from *The Sound of Music* and *South Pacific* — and Lord Beaverbrook's own favourite, *The Jones Boys.*

O the Jones Boys! They built a mill on the side of a hill, And they work'd all night and they work'd all day, But they couldn't make that gosh darn sawmill pay.

The occasion was the magnificent eighty-fifth birthday party given for Lord Beaverbrook by fellow Canadian Lord Thomson of Fleet.

It took place twenty years ago at the Dorchester Hotel in London.

There was a seven-tier birthday cake — seven tiers because seven was Lady Beaverbrook's lucky number.

Each tier represented a milestone in the life of Lord Beaverbrook.

The first marked his birth on May 25, 1879.

The second denoted that he was a Member of Parliament for Ashton-under-Lyne from 1910 to 1916.

The third recalled the First World War, when Lord Beaverbrook was the Canadian government representative on the Western Front, and later Minister of Information.

The fourth recorded newspaper history, when Lord Beaverbrook took over the *Daily Express* and founded the *Sunday Express* in 1918.

The fifth recalled the Second World War, when Lord Beaverbrook was Minister of Aircraft Production (1940-1942) and Member of the Cabinet until 1945.

The sixth tier marked Lord Beaverbrook's chancellorship of the University of New Brunswick in 1947 and his honorary chancellorship in 1957.

The seventh and top tier wished the guest of honour a Happy Birthday — 25 May, 1964.

It was, in short, one of the most lavish and memorable birthday parties ever given anywhere for anyone.

Lord Thomson of Fleet was determined it would be the most spectacular dinner in London's memory. And so it was, some claiming it was the most spectacular dinner in a hundred years.

There were 658 guests but those who were there still considered it an intimate dinner.

It was a dinner that almost did not happen.

At least, the guest of honour almost did not get to his eighty-fifth birthday party.

On that morning, Lord Beaverbrook, mortally ill with cancer, was told he must not leave his bed.

But leave it he did to appear that night at the Dorchester, to refuse a wheelchair that had been offered to him, and to walk the long walk through the dining room to his seat at the top table, where he soon would deliver one of the finest speeches of his life.

It was a night on which Lord Beaverbrook would call, for a short period, on the strength and zest of his long-departed youth. It was a night of raw courage and determination that characterized his life. It was a night when Lord Beaverbrook would demonstrate, once again, and for the final time, why he had been known throughout his life as a Master of Words.

The date was May 25, 1964. Fifteen days later, on June 9, 1964, Lord Beaverbrook was dead.

On that date, Fleet Street of London lost one of its most dynamic figures.

The world lost the man who in so many ways had helped turn the tide of history by producing the planes that won the Battle of Britain, and New Brunswick lost a great friend and a magnificent benefactor.

I was among the group of Canadians who attended Lord Beaverbrook's eighty-fifth birthday party, and the memories of that night are memories of a masterful performance by an old man, so close to death and yet so fiercely determined that he would give this, his final valedictory.

Later, although he only lived for two weeks, he was to write to me — and undoubtedly to many others — to thank me for attending his birthday party and to say he had hoped to see some of his Canadian friends on the afternoon of his birthday but had spent the whole day writing and rewriting his speech — "and even then it was too long."

But of course, it wasn't too long.

At the time of my return to Canada, I wrote about that evening at the Dorchester Hotel, and these are the words I used:

> There was a blare of trumpets and an old man entered the crowded ballroom of London's Dorchester Hotel.
>
> He walked slowly and used a cane to take some of the

pressure off the legs that had carried him with strong and fierce determination from his boyhood home in Newcastle, N.B., to the pinnacle of world fame and a secured place in history.

Now these once-driving limbs were tired, plagued with the gout and protesting the long walk to the head table, but they would not fail him on this night.

He had the stooped, rounded shoulders of a man of eighty-five. Much of the old-time vigour was gone, but none of the determination. He smiled as guests rose to give him a table-thumping ovation.

It was a wide smile, a mischievous and impish smile. It was a smile that is known around the world. His eyes were tired and heavy as he entered the ballroom, but they lit up and sparkled as he recognized old friends, old rivals — and some old enemies.

The Beaver had arrived.

Few who were privileged to be present will ever forget the scene. No one is likely to forget the remarkable speech that was to follow.

The occasion was this week's eighty-fifth birthday party given for Lord Beaverbrook by his fellow peer, newspaper magnate, and friend, Lord Thomson of Fleet.

Lord Thomson said, "This dinner is my personal tribute to the man who has shown me great friendship.

"To me he is the great professional."

Those present were in full agreement. They had known Lord Beaverbrook on Fleet Street, in politics, and in business, and they were present to pay tribute to "the great professional." And the Old Man, never one to shirk the spotlight, basked in the warmth of their greeting.

In the *Sunday Express* on the eve of the great party A.J.P. Taylor had written of Lord Beaverbrook's eternal optimism. In that article Taylor said, "Lord Beaverbrook has believed in life, rich and full, for himself and for others. His central decisive quality is: Zest.

"He has scattered this Zest broadcast. It is thanks to this Zest that our country is a brighter, more lively place.

"People often ask: what good has Lord Beaverbrook done?

"The answer is simple: he has done good as the sun does. He has shone."

So one again Lord Beaverbrook was shining in happiness and enthusiasm and undoubtedly laughing a bit to himself because he can appreciate the fact that few share the joy of attending their own eighty-fifth birthday gatherings. So Lord Beaverbrook's eyes twinkled as he sat centre stage, and his personality shone through the huge gathering. It was not his greatest hour. That, the world believes, had been in the Battle of Britain. But certainly it was a memorable hour — for Lord Beaverbrook and for many who had come from scattered parts of the world to pay him tribute.

They called the night Fleet Street's greatest tribute to any one man. Tributes came from Lord Thomson, Lord Rothermere, from Churchill, and the Duke of Windsor, whose voice had not been heard on the BBC for twenty-seven years, sent a warm and personal message to his "long-standing, tried and trusted friend." The message was read at the dinner and a recording made in New York was broadcast by the BBC.

But the man of the night was Lord Beaverbrook himself.

Lord Rothermere, chief proprietor of London's Daily Mail, which is nothing if it has not been a rival of Lord Beaverbrook's Express, recalled that his father, the first Lord Rothermere, said to him many years ago, "Poor Max — he has very bad health. Max will never make old bones."

The audience laughed.

Lord Rothermere added, "He was bang wrong in that." Again the audience laughed. Lord Beaverbrook roared. His sense of humour was still intact.

Then it was time for Lord Beaverbrook.

He is an old man. He is eighty-five. He is entering his eighty-sixth year, but he is entering it as another great adventure, and he told his audience, "In my eighty-sixth year I do not feel greatly different from my eighty-fifth.

"But," he added, "I am old bones. They are very weak. But I still have something in the way of a head. I still have some drive."

And for half an hour the audience was treated to touches of Lord Beaverbrook's mind, his drive, his worldly wisdom and warmth, but mostly it was the humour of this giant of this or any other generation—a giant of finance, journalism, the letters, the world of art, and a champion of the little man. Here was the man whose London Express reaches all classes in England and here was the Little Canadian, as he is sometimes called, recalling his early days, his great ambitions and disappointments and claiming he had never been anything more than an apprentice in any field he had entered.

The years rolled away as he spoke. His voice grew firmer, and a marvelling audience listened to a speech delivered with a vigour that would have been more characteristic of a man of thirty-five or forty.

Looking back on his life, he said, "I have never been a successful leader.

"I have always been an apprentice and never a master, and that has been my weakness in my political activities."

When he first arrived in Britain from Canada, he said, he was an apprentice to the House of Commons, then apprentice to Prime Minister Lloyd George, then apprentice to journalism.

He concluded: "It is time for me to become an apprentice once more. I am not certain in which direction, but somewhere, sometime, soon."

Never a leader? Many in the room disagreed.

But Lord Beaverbrook moved on.

He compared himself to his boyhood idol, the first Marquis of Montrose, who was hanged in 1630.

"Both of us came to failure after initial success. Both were let down.

"Montrose was let down by the Earl of Home...I was let down by Sir Alex Douglas Home's predecessor. But I was not let down at the end of a rope."

Another idol was remembered. It was Canada's Prime Minister Sir John A. Macdonald. Lord Beaverbrook had been greatly impressed by Sir John's splendid oratory, "but it would be easy for me to make a better speech than he at eighty-five—because he died at seventy-six."

What had led Lord Beaverbrook to Fleet Street?

The Beaver had part of the answer:

It had been said his boyhood home of Newcastle was too small for him. He had gone to Halifax, and the Nova Scotia city, they said, was too small for him. So it was on to Montreal, then a city of a quarter of a million, but Montreal was too small. London was his next stop, and London, it had been said, was too small for him.

But never fear, soon he would go to hell.

The audience roared. But The Beaver hadn't finished.

Eyes now sparkling and grin spreading, he said, "Hell will be too small, too."

Was all this an indication that The Beaver was thinking about the next world? Well, he's a realist and he's eighty-five. His earlier reference to a new apprenticeship "somewhere, sometime, soon" had been so straight-faced that it fooled some veteran newspapermen. Some actually thought he was considering a new worldly career.

He wasn't. The Beaver of Fleet Street just wanted his friends to know he is facing whatever lies ahead with a smile on his lips, that old mischievous and impish twinkle in his eyes—and a lot of curiosity.

All of that was years ago. Yet, in New Brunswick, his presence remains strong and it's all around us. He is gone but his good works and his vision are everywhere to behold. There are the buildings, the rinks, the monuments, the magnificent art gallery at Fredericton, and the Playhouse, which was a joint gift to the province from Lord Beaverbrook and his boyhood and lifelong friend, Sir James Dunn.

The greatest monument to Lord Beaverbrook, and to his association with and his love for New Brunswick, has to be the campus of the University of New Brunswick, which expanded and grew dramatically under his dynamic guidance during the years he was chancellor and later honorary chancellor.

All of this causes one to wonder if New Brunswick has done enough to honour and perpetuate the memory of this unusual man who loved New Brunswick with a great and unyielding passion, this man who altered history when he was asked by Churchill to produce the planes that would turn back Hitler's Nazi horde in an epic battle that changed the course of history more than a half-century ago.

−30−

Beaverbrook, Lady Dunn, and Cupid
— September 1959

— — — — — — —
— — — — —
—

LADY DUNN WAS FURIOUS.

She wanted to kill Lord Beaverbrook.

Figuratively speaking.

"Tell him," she said, "that I don't want my name mentioned ever again in connection with the art gallery. Do you hear me?" she demanded. "Yes," I said.

She was in St. Andrews. I was in Saint John. We were talking on the telephone, although I'm not certain that a telephone line was necessary.

She was shouting her instructions.

This was the fall of 1959 and what had upset Lady Dunn was a report that had appeared in the provincial newspapers about the new Beaverbrook Art Gallery in Fredericton. The article quoted Lord Beaverbrook, who praised "three ladies whose efforts have done more to grace the art gallery than I have myself."

The first lady mentioned was Lady Dunn, who had made numerous gifts to the gallery through the Sir James Dunn Foundation. Lord Beaverbrook made special reference to the "great Santiago El Grande by the surrealist painter Salvador Dali, which dominates the main entrance hall. The giant-sized work with its great steed bearing St. James aloft against a blue sky with cathedral-like vaulting was a subject of endless controversy, admiration, and criticism." But, said Lord Beaverbrook, it also was one of universal attraction for gallery visitors.

Lord Beaverbrook was lavish in his praise of Lady Dunn, her donations to the gallery, and her personal interest and involvement in hanging paintings and decorating the gallery.

However, he ran afoul of Her Ladyship when in the same report he made reference to "other ladies" who had made contributions to the gallery. One such donation was that of an "incomparable assortment of rare china" by Mrs. Howard Pillow of Montreal and St. Andrews, widow of a former president of the British American Bank Note Company.

Lady Dunn, who had indeed made many priceless contributions to the gallery, in addition to giving it much of her personal time, saw the Pillow collection as a "few teacups and saucers."

She felt slighted.

She held Lord Beaverbrook responsible.

"Tell him," she said again, "that I am never to be mentioned — never, never, never — in any story about the gallery."

I said I would convey the message to Beaverbrook.

At the time, I was managing editor of the Saint John newspapers. Lady Dunn had called in a towering rage. She wanted to speak to the publisher.

The publisher of the day, T.F. Drummie, was not available so the call was directed to my office. After hearing her out, I called Lord Beaverbrook, who was on one of his regular fall visits to Fredericton.

Lord Beaverbrook was eighty, still sharp and perceptive. He got the message.

His answer was very simple:

"Tell the dear lady I agree. It was thoughtless of me. Whatever she wishes is fine with me. She may have anything she wants. I agree with her."

He didn't go into detail. He didn't apologize. He said he agreed with her.

I dutifully called Lady Dunn and gave her Lord Beaverbrook's message.

She received it calmly and thanked me.

The matter was behind them. Lady Dunn had made her point. They were friends again.

And, as Lord Beaverbrook had said, "She may have anything she wants."

As it turned out, what she wanted, now that Jimmy Dunn was gone, was Lord Beaverbrook himself.

Lady Dunn did not want Lord Beaverbrook as an enemy. She wanted him as a friend, and eventually as her husband.

She got him. They were married June 7, 1963.

There was yet another sequel to the story. On September 25, 1959, the day after I had found myself acting as a mediator — or perhaps even as cupid — in this high-powered, behind-the-scenes drama, Lady Dunn sent me a warm note of appreciation. It read, "Dear Mr. Costello: I wish to express my thanks to you for your prompt attention yesterday — it showed a refreshing side of the profession — since it proved great consideration, courtesy and diplomacy. Believe me to be extremely grateful. Very sincerely, M.A. Dunn."

Very thoughtful, of course, but that was not all. Lady Dunn wanted to thank me in a more tangible way. So she placed another call to the publisher and this time she got through. She wanted my address.

"Why?" Mr. Drummie wanted to know.

"Because," she said, "I'm going to send him a case of champagne. He's wonderful."

Mr. Drummie: "You can't do that!"

Lady Dunn: "I can't? Why not?"

Mr. Drummie: "Because he's important to the newspaper and if you send him the champagne he'll probably start drinking and I'd be running everything by myself."

(It would be less than gracious of me to suggest Mr. Drummie was envious of all the attention and praise I was receiving from Lady Dunn, so I will refrain from doing so.)

It therefore was obvious, at least as the publisher inferred, that Lady Dunn was dealing with a confirmed alcoholic.

She understood.

But still she wanted my address. She would not send me champagne. She would send me flowers.

And she did. Two dozen red roses.

How did I learn of the Lady Dunn-Drummie conversation? Mr. Drummie himself told me. About a year later. He thought it was a great joke. I didn't.

John Fisher: The Man from Frosty Hollow, N.B.

———————
—————
—

A LOT OF LIFE, verve, enthusiasm, old-time hucksterism, and, in so many ways, a lot of sunshine went out of Canada with the death of New Brunswick's John Fisher.

He was called Mr. Canada, and I doubt that anyone ever challenged his right to such an unusual and all-encompassing title. He was a writer, after-dinner speaker, and commentator. He was a promoter. But above all he was a storyteller.

John Fisher hailed from the small community of Frosty Hollow, on the outskirts of Sackville. He attended Rothesay Collegiate School and got his law degree from Dalhousie University before embarking on a career as a salesman or missionary for Canada.

And, oh, how he loved to preach the gospel according to John—John Fisher, that is. The story of Canada was a lifelong passion for John Fisher.

In full flight and full voice, he was something to behold—his voice rising like the mighty tides of Fundy, rumbling like thunder or wafting like a soft breeze through a grove of maple trees in his native New Brunswick just before a summer shower. Yes, John Fisher could bring on the thunder and he could make the lightning flash. For years he did it on radio, speaking with breathless and captivating enthusiasm, his words bubbling forth and tumbling one after the other in a joyous cadence of rhythm, music, and power.

When John Fisher talked about New Brunswick, it was a land and province of weather-beaten wooden hay barns, and wooden bridges — covered bridges. But not just covered bridges. John Fisher talked about bridges so that you could see and feel and smell them.

John Fisher, with his breathless and breathtaking enthusiasm, would take you on a drive or a stroll through those bridges and tell you about the longest one in the world, "more than half a mile long," he used to say, about the bridge at Hartland. The bridges were covered to keep out the snow, "but those bridges would long be remembered by the village swain walking with a loved one . . . and what could be more romantic than a stroll through a covered bridge?"

John Fisher would pause for effect and then he would take his listeners back to their youth. "Ah, what nostalgic memories those bridges have for New Brunswickers."

John Fisher didn't see what ordinary mortals saw when they drove around New Brunswick. He saw and remembered snake fences, tote roads, singing lumberjacks, and pulp cutters. It was a province where he ate shad and called it "the most delicious fish that swims." It was a province of gaspereau and samphire greens, which grew in the marshes, and fiddleheads, "which look like sleepy ferns on the flooded meadowlands along the mighty St. John River."

I remember meeting John Fisher more than thirty years ago. The Chignecto Canal, that marvellous waterway that was to cut through the Isthmus of Chignecto near the New Brunswick-Nova Scotia border, was being promoted, and he had been brought to Saint John to put some additional fire into the campaign.

He was, without question, the man for the job. Heck, John Fisher could bring an audience to a fever pitch just talking about digging a well or picking blueberries.

My involvement, by the way, was that of a reporter. I was going to cover John Fisher's speech, and I needed to get some advance information because he would still be speaking when the afternoon newspaper went to press.

As fate would have it, John Fisher wanted to see me, too. In fact, he said, he'd be happy to see me that morning. Perhaps I'd be good enough to bring along some newspaper clippings about the Chignecto Canal. He wanted to check out a few facts.

So that is how and why I arrived at the Admiral Beatty Hotel that long ago morning, laden down with newspaper clippings about the Chignecto Canal.

When John Fisher greeted me at his hotel room, it was apparent that he had entertained old friends the night before. The room had all the telltale signs of visitors who had arrived early and stayed late. Stale smoke hung heavily in the room. The glasses and trays told the rest of the story.

John Fisher found me a chair and cleared a corner of a small table. "I hope you'll excuse things," he said, with something of a shrug or shudder of resignation, "we had a bit of a reunion last night."

But now it was one of those by-the-dawn's-ugly-light mornings. It was 10:15 and John Fisher was to meet his luncheon hosts at 12 noon.

"Well," he said, "I guess there's work to be done. What did you bring?"

It was at this point that I realized he did not have a prepared speech. In fact, he had no speech whatsoever. He wasn't worried. He knew the story of the Chignecto Canal. He knew what his audience wanted to hear, but still the morning was slipping away.

Not to worry. Within moments he was flipping through the newspaper clippings, making notes, trying phrases in that deep, resonant voice that was known to hundreds of thousands of Canadians.

By 11:30 he had made enough notes to give him the flow that he wanted. And later that day, at about 1:30, he rose to his feet in the ballroom of the Admiral Beatty Hotel, took out the notes he had written only two hours earlier on the backs of envelopes, and launched into another of his virtuoso speaking performances.

Half an hour later he was given a standing ovation by an audience that had been thrilled not only by his command of the language and his faultless delivery, but also by his intimate knowledge of history and the unquestioned value of the Chignecto Canal. Alas, it was never built.

As John Fisher and the head table marched out of the ballroom, the audience once again standing and applauding, he spotted me at the press table. John Fisher smiled, nodded—and winked.

He was quite a guy, John Fisher was.

Miller Brittain: The Agony and the Ecstasy

— — — — — — —
— — — — —
—

MILLER BRITTAIN was settled comfortably in the corner of a soft
chesterfield chair, his legs somehow gathered beneath him so that he almost
appeared to be folded like an accordion or a boneless teddy bear.

He drank and smoked and talked. He argued. He smiled, laughed, slapped his
legs, and pounded the table. He jerked upright to make a point and then settled
back to listen, but not for long. He jabbed his finger for emphasis, wrapped his
arms around his own little frame, and laughed and laughed and laughed.

Miller Brittain was an animated conversationalist: a performing conversationalist.

This is the Miller Brittain I remember, the Miller Brittain who could be warm
and charming, an engaging and stimulating conversationalist and debater—and
not yet a troubled and raging figure driving himself to the brink and beyond
the brink of reality.

Miller Brittain, in those days when I knew him best, was often the centre
of attention, the centre of conversation. He laughed a lot in those happy days.
Laughed and giggled. Sometimes the giggle was more of a cackle, but even then
it could be warm, genuine, and infectious. These were the days when Miller
Brittain would spend time at the Air Force Club on Sydney Street, where the
1880 Club was later located. He had no worldly wealth, no money to speak

of, hardly enough to squeeze by on, but he had his own brilliance, his own genius.

And the demons had not yet started their work, or at least their work was not apparent, except that on occasions Miller Brittain could be completely unfathomable, unpredictable, and outrageous.

These were the days when lives were being rearranged, restructured, and started over again. Miller Brittain was one of those who had interrupted a promising career as an artist to go overseas with the R.C.A.F. He was a veteran of thirty-seven bombing missions over Europe and the holder of the Distinguished Flying Cross. He was a war hero.

Those were the days when the air force veterans were still young men, when they still relived their days in the service, and when the newly acquired and very busy Air Force Club kept them young. These were the times when you could find the Bardsley brothers — Bob and Jack — at the club quarters. Phil Connell and Norm Jackson, David Lunney, Ed Fitzgerald, Joe Richards, Don Welsford, and many others. And Miller Brittain.

Kingsley Brown, the onetime managing editor of this newspaper, was on the scene for a couple of years. He had been a prisoner of war, and he was among those who could talk and drink the night away and be on duty the next day at the crack of dawn.

It was not unusual at that time in the history of Saint John for a party to move from the Air Force Club to the Brittain home on Sewell Street, an apartment where you would wend your way through a clutter of furniture, boxes, paintings, and a piano that also served as a stand-up lunch counter and centre-of-the-room location for singers, talkers, and drinkers.

It was an apartment where you could find last week's unfinished meals almost any place — on the piano, on chairs, and uncooked on the back of the stove. Paintings were everywhere, in every stage of development.

It was obvious that a dog had full run of the Brittain home and it was equally obvious that, when nature called, the dog did not know the difference between the value of yesterday's newspaper and a painting that today could bring a price of $20,000. This was the home of Miller Brittain, artist.

This was a time when Miller Brittain was still waiting for the recognition he craved and deserved. It was a time when his voice would rage about bloody Upper Canadians and dip in despair and anger.

He had a voice that screamed like the wind as he challenged the establishment or ridiculed and mimicked friends and foes alike.

Now, suddenly, it is years later and I am listening once again to the voice of Miller Brittain. I am sitting in my own home and Miller Brittain is talking. But not in the same voice. It is not the voice of a man who has already lived most of his life. It is the voice of a man who has been dragged through the wringer of life and has not been able to cope with its challenges because coping would have meant bending to the will of others, or accepting the values of others, or compromising his own principles and his own will. Miller Brittain was not prepared to live by the rules of others because that would have meant compromising his principles, his very soul.

So I close my eyes and try to remember the voice of Miller Brittain as I listen to the small record, which is an excerpt from a National Film Board program of 1963. Miller Britain is talking seriously, slowly, and ponderously about his life, about his roots, and about how he must do things his own way. It is a tired voice coming from the depths of a man old before his time. It is a sad voice.

This is Miller Brittain talking about painting in 1963: "It's something you feel and almost seems to take over . . . it's pushing out into the unknown and . . . .

"It is a religious thing. You must believe when that happens that . . . . I began when I studied in New York many years ago. I worked in black and white and any painting techniques I've developed on my own. Most of the paintings and drawings start off as abstractions but always come to terms with nature around us. For instance, the human figure and landscape, natural forms . . . .

"But in every case they start off with simply shape and colour. Even the most realistic of my paintings. Some have called it surrealism, others expressionism.

"The general buying public thinks in terms of schools as also do the critics, and I'm afraid that I must proceed on my own way as I've always done. I'm not the kind of painter who can move from one place to another and work. I have to have my roots in. Our people came here after the American Revolution and my roots are very, very definitely here."

That was Miller Brittain, but it was not the Miller Brittain I would want to remember.

But now once again I can hear his voice, his real voice — even though it is not on a record and not on tape. But it is Miller Brittain's voice, vibrant, challenging, a laughing, giggling, joyous voice. I can hear Miller Brittain the mimic, and a moment later the bitter, chip-on-the-shoulder voice. I can see the hurt and sadness in his eyes.

Once again I can see his mannerisms as he slaps his knee in great fits of laughter or in anger and frustration.

This is Miller Brittain in full flight as he savages a non-buyer who wants to tell Miller Brittain what is wrong with his work, why it is non-commercial.

"Why do you have to make all the people look so sad?"

This is Miller Brittain mimicking one of the viewers of a Toronto exhibition which had been a failure — a failure because Miller Brittain believed there was a huge conspiracy against Maritime artists in general and Miller Brittain in particular.

Miller Brittain again: "For God's sake, if the face isn't wearing a stupid smile or the colour doesn't match her walls ... what the hell did they think it was ... Woolworth's?"

Now Miller Brittain is in a rage. This is the Miller Brittain with both rum and fire in his gut. This is the Miller Brittain who is ready to fight the world.

"And your National Gallery," he sneers.

The National Gallery had it in for Miller Brittain. He was convinced they had put out the word to blackball him. Harry Orr McCurry, the National Gallery's director from 1939 until 1955, was the culprit. This was the same McCurry who, in Brittain's opinion, had created "the tyranny of the Group of Seven" — the same McCurry who was instrumental in steering the Canadian art establishment in that direction.

Miller Brittain hated McCurry.

He had no love for Alan Jarvis, who succeeded McCurry. "He's from the tree-and-landscape school. Besides, he's a damn Christian Scientist and hates my guts because I'm not a teetotaller like him."

Miller Brittain, the boy artist of the Depression Years. Miller Brittain, war hero and war artist. Miller Brittain, the handsome and brilliant artist who had acquired nothing of material value in his most productive years. Nothing but his genius. This week I listened as the voice of Miller Brittain came out of the past to haunt me and remind me how much he was a part of the Saint John scene that now seems to be slipping away into a faded memory. Not only did I listen to the voice of Miller Brittain, I read his words and phrases, I sensed his anger and recalled his rage. And, at times, his humour.

All of this, the life and style, the work, the joy and anger, and, ultimately, the tragedy of Miller Brittain, is captured in an innovative and imaginative book entitled *Miller Brittain in Focus*, which records much of the life of Miller Brittain and in doing so touches the life and fabric of Saint John and the people of Saint John. It contains reproductions of much of the work of the artist and then branches off to include as well a reproduction of the tunic of Miller Brittain's R.C.A.F. uniform, which contains another surprise when opened — to reveal the letter written to Flying Officer M.G. Brittain when he was awarded the Distinguished Flying Cross.

There is more. Much, much more. The book captures the sense and the style and the heart and the soul of Miller Brittain. You see once again the little, balled-up, formless, grinning pixie all but disappearing in a chair behind a table lined with bottles, glasses, cups, and jars — anything that people would drink from when a party was on. The book brings back some of the raging and tormented tornado of a man possessed.

It is not simply the story of Miller Brittain. It is the story of an artist and the art colony of Saint John in the grim and forbidding 1930s, the horrible days of the Great Depression. It is the story of war in the skies over Europe and the men who returned from that war.

It is a story that touches, often only briefly but with deep perception, on life in Saint John. It is the story of struggling artists and of the powerful and the things that shaped the times of Miller Brittain.

It is the story of Miller Brittain and Jack Humphrey and Fred Ross. Fred Ross was younger, and the story records how Miller liked the young artist and wanted to help him, but didn't appreciate the competition that was represented in a developing talent. ("How long is that kid going to be twenty-one years old?" Miller would ask his friends.)

It is the story of Miller Brittain and Jim Stackhouse, of Ted Campbell and Avery Shaw, and Jean Sweet, Norman Cody, and many others in and on the fringe of the artistic community.

It is a love story: Miller Brittain's love for Connie Starr, and his love for and devotion to their daughter Jennifer — and how death so swiftly robbed him of both of them, Connie's death snatching her away and Miller's own death taking him from the daughter he adored.

There is another side to the love story. It is the love that so many people gave to Miller Brittain. It is the story of those who tried so desperately to save him from himself, the record of those who tried to ward off the demons that were to consume Miller Brittain.

The Carters — Norwood and Margaret Ann — tried to help him, to save him. So did the Millers, Doug as a doctor and a friend. Paul and Celia Toomik fought the losing battle for years, right up to the very end. It was not a fight they could win. The demons were too strong, the artist too weak. They could prolong the fight, but they could not win it.

In the end, they lost Miller Brittain but salvaged much of his work. And now, in *Miller Brittain in Focus*, another valuable insight into the man and his work is captured and preserved.

−30−

Remembering Marita

– – – – – – –
– – – – –
–

FOR YEARS HER NAME was a household word in Saint John. Marita. Marita McNulty.

She was that lively, vivacious, sparkling personality of radio—the one who conducted the *Meet Me In The Market* broadcast.

The program, as the name suggested, originated at the City Market and featured many of the colourful characters who were part of the daily scene at this landmark gathering place in the centre of the city.

Marita was more than a radio personality. She was a first-class news interviewer, a professional singer, a fashion commentator, and, for years, one of the favourites of those wonderful Saint John operettas produced by the Knights of Columbus.

She had a wide following as a singer and radio personality, and at one time was probably as well known and popular in Saint John as Andy Duffy, the famous police officer of an earlier generation who won recognition and fame directing traffic at the head of King Street.

I first knew Marita when she was young, when we all were young—when everyone was young except the old people. That was half a century ago.

I met Marita because I knew her brother Eddie. Ned Barrett. He and I started out together as a couple of teenage reporters.

He was the smart one. The ambitious one. He went on to hold senior editorial positions with the *Montreal Herald* and the *Montreal Star*. They were great newspapers in their day — the *Herald* a lively tabloid, the *Star* one of Canada's most successful and respected newspapers of record.

But this isn't a story about Ned Barrett. It's about Marita, and I'm writing it because Ned told me recently that she hadn't been well. That, in turn, got me thinking about those years so long ago, half a century ago, when friends would gather in the Barrett home on Wellington Row.

Those were particularly happy times, I remembered — though for the life of me I don't know what that family, the Barretts, had to be so happy about.

They had seen better times. The father had been a successful business man, and the Depression came along and he was successful no longer. The mother had a debilitating illness that sapped her strength but never her spirit, even though she would live the final years of her life as a cripple.

Yet they were plucky, the Barretts were. Plucky and game, a family that believed that adversity was there only so you could face it down, spit in its eye, and get on with your life. There was a lot of laughter, much music, and a great mountain of happiness in the Barrett home.

There were others in the family. Bill and Dianne, Elizabeth and Caroline. Eventually they all left Saint John, and some years ago Bill and then Dianne left this world.

Marita was the one who stayed longest in Saint John. She married a handsome naval officer at the end of the war. At least I remember him as being much-beribboned and handsome. I suppose he was. Alas, the marriage did not last, but from that day on Marita Barrett was Marita McNulty.

She became one of Saint John's best-known radio personalities, probably rivalling the popularity of Uncle Bill (Hugh Trueman) and his Junior Radio Stars and Jene Wood — who took over that program after Trueman left.

Marita McNulty's *Market* program drew not only Saint John listeners, but avid followers from around the province and Nova Scotia. They would flock to the City Market to see the broadcast, many of them in the hope of being interviewed — and many of them were.

Ned Barrett recalled recently the farmer from Cambridge, a grandfather with a fine voice and a big family, who invited Marita to his home to join in a family hymn sing after Sunday service.

Word spread about the trip and on Monday morning there was an eager audience waiting to hear her program — and the great songs of faith coming from an old Loyalist home where the farmer lived.

Marita, whose reputation as a concert singer had long been established, found herself acclaimed as a Gospel singer, and her taped "hymn a day" from the farmer's home became a favourite of her program.

When the station decided the hymns had run their course, listeners rebelled, and Marita was astounded when she received a telephone call from Bishop Leverman.

He urged her to continue the hymns because somehow, inexplicably, there were people who thought he opposed them. He was being blamed for having them banned. The hymn sings went back on the air. The popularity of the program continued.

Marita studied voice for six years under Alfreda Kukainis, but her singing career probably began as a soloist at wartime weddings of countless friends. When she introduced "Ave Maria" as part of one of Saint John's wartime troupe shows, there were those who wondered whether a sacred song was appropriate for a lively crowd of soldiers and merchant seamen.

They need not have worried. After her performance there was no doubt it would be heard again and again and would become an all-time favourite of those shows for the servicemen.

Her last major appearance in Saint John was in 1967 as Amneris in the New Brunswick Opera Company's *Aida*, a production that was acclaimed as one of the city's finest musical presentations.

And then, shortly after, Marita left the *Market* broadcast, left Radio CFBC and Saint John.

She moved to Charlottetown, where she became public relations director of Prince of Wales College, soon to amalgamate with St. Dunstan's to become the University of Prince Edward Island.

Soon she was as active in Charlottetown as she had been in Saint John. She did a weekly broadcast of *University Magazine* on Radio CFCY, later a weekly broadcast of classical music and opera selections on Radio CHTN.

She became a member of the board of the Community Concert Association, a member of the Prince Edward Island Garden Club, the Prince Edward Island Council of the Arts, the Sherwood Beautification Committee, and an enthusiastic supporter of the visual and performing arts.

Eventually she retired from her position at the university, and that allowed her time to travel, which she did with great enthusiasm on a world scale, but never with more enthusiasm than when she made her annual summer pilgrimage to Grand Manan, the vacation spot she loved more than any other.

This summer, though, she did not visit Grand Manan. It had to be delayed and then cancelled. The persistent cough, she had been told, was not a cold. It was more serious. Much more serious.

The news was a shock for her family and friends, but Marita reacted much as her mother had before her. She accepted what she was told, spat once more in adversity's eye, and decided to get on with what was left of her life.

She would see friends as she always had, she would entertain as she had always done. She would continue as long as she had the energy to do so.

The friends came by the hundreds, from hundreds of miles away and from just across the street. They came, as her brother Ned put it so touchingly, "to say goodbye — without ever saying goodbye. No one wanted to believe that they were sharing a cup of tea with Marita for the last time."

And then one morning a chamber music trio that had been playing in Charlottetown, and had invited her as a special guest at their performance the night before, visited her at her home.

They came to perform a light concert in her living room. Some special friends were present. The musicians gave what they said was their own command performance. They played for forty minutes — and then left, racing to the airport just in time to catch their plane.

It was a visit and gesture that brought great happiness to Marita, who in her life had brought so much entertainment and so much happiness to others through her music.

It was another act of kindness, warmth, and affection from her friends in the world of music — an act she will remember as she continues, spirit still high, down the path that for Marita, and for all of us, grows shorter with each passing day.

Others Saw Clouds and Rain, He Saw Rainbows

------- ----- -

HE WAS A KNIGHT of the Open Road. A cheerful, humorous free spirit of the highways. He carried a bag. He called on the trade. He was a travelling man. He smiled a lot and told stories. He had a sense of humour that knew no bounds.

He was a dreamer. There was always a rainbow in the sky and a pot of gold at the end of the rainbow. Someday, he would find that pot of gold.

He never did, but that didn't stop him from dreaming. It didn't dampen his spirits or discourage him. He was an optimist. He had a heart as big as his smile, and his smile was as large as all outdoors.

He should have been on the stage. In the movies. On radio and television. He loved sport and could have been a sports writer or a commentator on radio or television. He also should have been just what he was — a travelling man. A commercial traveller.

His name was Gordon Stults, and he crammed a lot of happiness into his fifty-nine years — happiness for himself and for others. Gordon Stults had tunnel vision. He could only see the bright side of things — even when there was no bright side. Others would see clouds and rain. Gordon would see the rainbow.

He was a storyteller. He laughed at himself and he laughed at the world. He laughed when others would have cried. He laughed when others were crying for him and his misfortunes.

He made others, who were much more fortunate, feel inadequate. And then he made them feel fortunate—fortunate that they would see the sun come up the next day, fortunate that they had so many things to be thankful for. In a wheelchair, he could make the healthy feel envious of his good humour, his unconquerable spirit, his will to live, and his willingness to enjoy life as it came.

He told stories and made quips when death was near, when time was running out, when he had only months, perhaps weeks, to live. He laughed and joked and searched out the brightness of life right up until the end.

Finally, in the last weeks, it would be little more than a wry comment or a flip remark, but the world had been his stage and he continued to perform as long as he had the strength to do so. He was not in a hurry to take his final bow, and his final exit.

Years ago on a vacation trip to Boston we had a taxi driver who was trying to find a late-night bistro for us. We thought we were thirsty and in need of something to sustain us. Gordon was in full flight in the back seat of the cab. Finally, the driver pulled over to the curb. Tears were running down his face. "You've got to stop it, Mister," he said, "or we're going to have an accident."

Gordon didn't stop, but somehow the driver managed to find an all-night Chinese restaurant before collapsing from laughter.

"Are you on the stage, Mister?" the taxi driver wanted to know.

Gordon said he wasn't. He was a brain surgeon from Canada giving courses to surgeons in Boston—and he wanted to do all his drinking that night because he was in the operating room at 6 a.m. the next morning.

The driver drove off into the night still shaking with laughter and we entered the restaurant. Alas, the restaurant was open but the bar was closed. It was after hours, the owner told us.

He could serve us food but not liquor.

That, for Gordon Stults, was like throwing an anchor to a drowning man.

Putting his arm around the restaurant owner, he confided that I was a man of great influence, a government agent from Canada, on an important case in Boston (Gordon just made the stories up as he went along), and the Canadian government would appreciate if it I could be accommodated.

The owner didn't buy that one.

"What if we get a special dispensation from the mayor?" The owner shook his head. "It's too late. I'd lose my licence."

"What if I had a special letter from the Pope?" Gordon didn't want to leave any card unplayed. Who knows? This Chinese restaurant owner might have converted to Catholicism.

"No, sorry," said the owner. He was adamant.

Finally, Gordon decided it was time to play his ace card. Lowering his voice to a stage whisper, he said, "I want to tell you something I've never told anyone else. I'm a personal friend of Chiang Kai-shek's and he told me to look you up if I was ever in Boston."

The restaurant owner bowed a deep and respectful bow. I'm not sure whether he was impressed or merely going along with the gag but he said he was very happy to meet a friend of Chiang Kai-shek's.

Gordon smiled that winning smile of his. "And now," he said, "how about a drink for me and my friends."

"Oh, no, sorry," said the owner. "It's after hours."

"Come on, Ralph," said Gordon. "That was my best shot. Let's go." And we did.

That's the way he went through life. You win some, you lose some, and then you move along to the next game. There's always another game, another challenge—another story to be told, and another laugh to be laughed.

Gordon Stults was not supposed to survive the stroke that felled him almost fifteen years ago. But he did. He beat the odds. After days and weeks of nothing, his eyes opened, he groped for and found words—and as soon as he could put words into sentences we knew he had not survived alone. His sense of humour was alive and well, too.

That sense of humour, the rare ability to find happiness in despair, would remain with him through all the years he had remaining on this earth. As recently as two weeks ago he was still on stage. In discomfort and pain and with the sands of time running even faster, he remained the storyteller. His arm was broken and in a special cast. He wanted the cast removed but first he had to convince the doctor.

It was more bother than it was worth, he said. Everyone was visiting his room to examine it.

"Everyone?" asked the doctor.

"Yes, everyone," said Gordon. "Everyone wants to take a crack at old Gord. I think someone is selling tickets at the door." They took the cast off.

Soon though, the final, fading spark left his eyes. The fight had been fought. The game was over. I stood at the foot of his bed and his dark eyes sought desperately to focus, to give a sign of recognition, but it was too late. There was nothing there. I picked up my coat to leave and as I did his lips moved. A voice, weak and raspy, forced itself through dry, parched lips. It was a voice of desperation and yet typically, one of care and concern.

It was a voice seemingly from the depths of hell. "Ralph," he said, "please don't go."

He wanted me to know that he knew I was there and that he cared.

I stayed for a while and then slipped away.

Two days later he did the same thing. He slipped away. He will be missed, but wherever he has gone will be a happier place for his presence.

−30−

Will the Irish Mafia Ever Cry Uncle?

THERE IS NO QUESTION about it. The Irish Establishment of Saint John was worried.

The Irish Establishment?

Yes, the Irish Establishment. Or call them the Irish Elite, or if you come from the other side of town and ride a white horse on July 12 you might call them the Irish Mafia.

Establishment, Elite, Mafia — it doesn't really matter. They are worried.

Hugh McLennan and Frank Ervin looked furtively and nervously about the room as if in search of some unwanted intruder. Norm Garey, Danny Britt, and Norm Harrington were in a corner carrying on one of those conversations in stage whispers.

The occasion was St. Patrick's Day, 1984, and a sense of foreboding gripped the entire gathering with such force that hardly anyone was able to get a glass to his lips without spilling the contents.

"She's going to do something," said Frank Ervin. "I just know it. She'll find a way."

"How do you know she's going to do something?" he was asked.

"I just know it, that's all. I feel it in my bones."

"But what can she do? She isn't invited. She wouldn't show up uninvited?"

"Don't bet on it," said John Mooney, his upper lip quivering nervously and sweat dripping from his chin. "She was some mad."

They were talking about Saint John mayor Elsie Wayne. She had waited patiently for her invitation to the annual St. Patrick's Dinner, and when it failed to arrive, she had taken the initiative by writing to the president.

"Should we read her letter at the dinner?" someone asked.

"Not on your life."

Councillor John Schermerhorn had been named the city's designated hitter when the mayor failed to get an invitation to the all-male dinner, and now the members of the Establishment began to eye him suspiciously.

"Well, if Councillor Schermerhorn is here, that means she isn't coming," said Norm Garey, but he didn't speak very convincingly.

"There's no way she could get in," said someone who obviously was not very well acquainted with the mayor.

"Wait a minute. Wait a minute. Is there a cake?" someone wanted to know.

"A cake?"

"Yes, a cake. A large cake. Is there a cake?"

"You don't think she'd . . . ." The voice trailed off. "No, she wouldn't dare."

There was silence.

Then, "You mean the old pop-out-of-the-cake trick?"

"Well, at least she'd wear her chains of office," said an officer of the St. Patrick's Society who will remain nameless forever.

There was laughter but it was weak and uncertain.

Finally, the huddle in the suite at the Delta Hotel broke up. They would ask councillor John Schermerhorn if he knew anything. Was the mayor planning anything tricky? Was he going to read her letter?

"No way," he replied with one of his larger-than-life smiles. "You can count on me, boys," he said and at the same time slapped Norm Garey on the back as a sign of friendship, knocking him momentarily to his knees.

Thinking Garey was praying for divine guidance, other members of the St. Patrick's executive quickly dropped to their knees beside him.

This was too much for me. "What's going on?" I demanded, thinking I might be witnessing some strange society rite associated with St. Patrick's Day and not wanting to be left out.

"It's nothing, Ralph," Garey told me as he struggled to his feet, quickly followed by the executive. "It's nothing you would understand. Just a little problem we've been having with the mayor. We were afraid she might have sent us a message through Councillor Schermerhorn, but he says he isn't going to read her letter or anything like that."

"You can count on me, boys," Councillor Schermerhorn shouted boisterously, winding up to give someone else a friendly slap on the back, but this time everyone ducked.

"Don't worry about it, Ralph," Frank Ervin repeated. "Just go over in the corner and practise your speech. It doesn't involve you."

"Okay," I said, repressing one of those cat-that-ate-the-canary smiles and looking dumb, which I do very effectively, I have been told. Then, just to be sure, I patted my breast pocket where I had the copy of the mayor's letter — the one that everyone was worried about.

So the plot thickens.

And thicken it did throughout the evening until Councillor Schermerhorn had finished his greetings from the city without mentioning anything of the mayor's challenge to the Saint John tradition of marking St. Patrick's Day with a stag dinner.

The individual and collective sighs of relief had subsided by the time I came to the middle of my speech, where it seemed appropriate to mention the mayor's letter.

There was really no way I could avoid it. Not after what I'd been through during the preceding week.

It all began when someone started slipping messages under the door of my office.

They were unsigned notes — but the message was clear and consistent.

"Did you know," the first one said, "that the mayor of the City of Saint John has not been invited to the St. Patrick's Day Dinner?"

Then there was one that read, "Are you going to address the group that has insulted the mayor of Saint John and all women of the city?"

One of the most surprising letters was not an original but a copy. It read, "Fred, see what you can do for Elsie." It was on official Vatican letterhead, and while the signature was unclear I got the impression that the letter was from someone very important.

This was a copy of a letter to Fred Hazel, who had visited an old Polish friend in Rome a few months earlier.

Finally there was a copy of a letter from Mayor Wayne to Fred Hazel. It said, "Fred, see if Ralph can get my message across."

That was the one that did it.

How could I be so ungallant as to refuse such a desperate last-ditch request from the mayor of the city?

On the other hand, I was a guest at the dinner, so there was the question of how far I should go. Finally, I decided I would read a couple of excerpts from the mayor's letter.

Here, in part, is what she said:

"My best wishes go out to you this evening as you hold your annual celebration commemorating St. Patrick and all that is grand and Irish.

"It, however, is my regret that there still exists, in our world, gatherings where the chief magistrate of the municipality will be excluded simply and only because that magistrate is a 'dame.'

"Although it is not to your credit, gentlemen, you are not the only order of Celts in Saint John to say no to the grey-haired old lady from City Hall on the meagre grounds of gender."

So there. That was the mayor's message, and I must say it was received with good grace by the audience. At least they didn't attack me with buns, as I am told they did one year when they were displeased with the speaker of the evening.

As to whether the St. Patrick's Society should open the meeting to, uh, members of the other gender, as the mayor put it — well, that was something for the society itself to decide.

I did, however, venture a couple of comments, suggesting that I myself would be a bit wary when Her Worship started describing herself as a harmless grey-haired old lady from City Hall.

That little old grey-haired lady from City Hall, I suggested, was about as harmless as a cobra poised to strike, and if you buy that little old lady line, well this is 1847 all over again and you've just landed on Partridge Island; you are weary, worn, ill, and crazed with the fever.

I suggested that the mayor might well have described herself just about the same way a few years ago when she became the voice of Glen Falls and champion of the people whose basements were being flooded.

Readers will recall she was on radio every morning cutting up the civic administration of the day, and someone got the idea that she might be establishing a political base. So she was asked if she had any political ambitions.

I understand she laughed and said, in effect, "who — little old me? Why I'm just a harmless little old grey-haired lady who wants to get the water out of her basement."

And then, almost overnight, she became so popular that she was in fact elected to the Common Council.

Yet, again if I recall it correctly, that didn't quite satisfy her and instead of thanking the politician whose radio station had helped launch her political career, she decided she'd take his job at City Hall.

And on election night, when the results were in, it seems to me that she said, "Gee whiz, I'm just a little old grey-haired lady who was running for the fun of it. I didn't really want to win."

So if I were going to give the St. Patrick's Society any advice — and I'm not — but if I were, I'd simply say they should never underestimate the determination of those little old ladies from Glen Falls.

The mayor claims to have Irish blood in her veins, so once through the door, once within the walls of the august chamber of Saint John's historic celebration of St. Patrick's Day, I can assume it would only be a matter of time until the president of the St. Patrick's Society would be — Elsie O'Wayne herself.

−30−

Joey Smallwood and an Audience of Three

—————
————
—

THE TWO MEN CHATTED BRIEFLY before catching their plane, where they did not sit together.

Later, at the Ottawa Airport, the Newfoundlander who was not a living legend was met by his wife and twelve-year-old daughter. At the baggage carousel he found himself standing next to Joey Smallwood and, on learning that the former premier was going to the Château Laurier, offered him a lift.

Now, if there are four people in an automobile and one of them is Joey Smallwood, that means the Living Legend has the pleasure of an audience of three. The Living Legend proceeded to address his captive audience.

Joey, as usual, was in good form, even though it quickly became apparent that he also was a bit perturbed. It could not be said that he was in a towering rage, but he was upset about some recent reports that had suggested Newfoundlanders who moved to the mainland were capable of handling only the most menial of jobs.

That, Joey trumpeted, simply was not true. Why, Newfoundland had sent some of its best brains to the mainland in an effort to help those less fortunate who had not had the good judgment and foresight to be born on the island. Newfoundland had provided Canada with outstanding business executives and entrepreneurs, doctors, lawyers, professors....

"Why," said Joey, "I understand the University of New Brunswick has just named a Newfoundlander as its president."

The other Newfoundlander in the car, who happened to be the president-designate of UNB, allowed himself only a silent smile and decided it would be immodest to confess to his identity.

Besides, it is difficult to get a word in when Joey Smallwood is in full flight.

But not if you are twelve years of age and the proud daughter of the new president of the University of New Brunswick.

"It's him...it's him," she all but shouted at the Living Legend. "It's him," she exclaimed, pointing to her father.

And that's how Joey Smallwood and Jim Downey, the new president of UNB, became more or less formally introduced.

James Downey, B.A., B.Ed., M.A., Ph.D., became the fourteenth president of the University of New Brunswick at ceremonies in Fredericton. I had the impression that the man had a sense of humour. In discharging his new responsibilities as president of UNB, it should have come in handy.

−30−

ABOUT THE IRVINGS

Jim Irving Visits the Mill with His Father

– – – – – – –
– – – – –
–

WHEN HE WAS WITHIN FIVE MONTHS of his ninetieth birthday, his interest in seeing wheels turn was as strong as ever.

With Jim he was making an unannounced night visit to Rothesay Paper, now their long-sought Saint John newsprint mill, soon to be renamed Irving Paper Limited. Together, they walked through the plant as newsprint was churned out in a never-ending production cycle. At the end of a long walk they entered a small office where Jim often stopped for a few minutes on his regular visits. It was hot in the mill, cooler in the shed-like cubicle. It was a place where someone kept a small container of eyeglass cleaner and, as was his habit, Jim polished his glasses with a couple of sheets of toilet paper, kept there for that purpose. Then he asked if his father would like his glasses cleaned.

"Why, yes, that would be fine," said K.C. Irving. He handed his glasses to his son, who squirted them and then pulled on the roll of toilet tissue and unwound, with a bit of flourish, about ten or twelve sheets.

"Jimmy, Jimmy, what are you doing?" his father asked, with more than a touch of alarm in his voice.

"I'm going to clean your glasses," his oldest son answered.

"Well, you're being a bit extravagant, aren't you?" asked the patriarch of the Irving family, looking in disapproval at the long ribbon of tissue.

Jim Irving, sixty years of age, quietly rewound the paper and tore off two sheets. He shined his father's glasses, returned them, and they left the mill.

Later, he told of the incident with pride in his eighty-nine-year-old father's sharpness. "He was as fast as a whip when he saw how much paper I was going to waste. No," said Jim Irving, approvingly, in answer to a question that hadn't been asked, "he isn't going to change. Not now. Not ever."

–30–

Art Irving Busts His Father Out of Hospital

— — — — — —
— — — —
—

AT NINETY-ONE he knew that his heart was not as strong as it once had been. He knew he should be taking it easy. What he didn't know was how to do it. How to slow down. His pace worried his family but there was little they could do about it, and on a day in late 1990 it came as no great surprise when he was taken exhausted to hospital in Saint John and later to the Lahey Clinic in Boston.

There he remained for six weeks in seclusion, confined to intensive care while his heart was monitored, while the media tried daily and persistently to learn something about his condition. The family was noncommittal, the hospital professionally vague in response to reporters' questions. The sons flew back and forth between Boston and Saint John, tight lipped and worried. Then, in his office in Saint John, Arthur received a telephone call.

"Is that you, Art?"

"Yes, Dad."

"Art, I'm in hospital and I want to get out."

"Are you feeling better, Dad?"

"Yes, and I want out of here."

"Well, Dad...."

"Today, Art. Get me out of this place."

Within an hour a plane was on its way to Boston. Kenneth Colin Irving checked out of the hospital, flew to Bermuda, and slept that night in his own bed. His body had grown old but nothing had weakened his will.

In private and in public he stressed that "The Boys" were "running her"—in charge of everything he had built and all the new businesses and industries they themselves had added to the vast conglomerate. That was the business side of it.

Kenneth Colin Irving, father, was another matter. In the family, he was loved, respected, revered, and in the family circle he was still the boss. "The Boys" would have it no other way.

−30−

Do You Have Your Long Johns On?

— — — — — — —
— — — — —
—

"DO YOU HAVE YOUR LONG JOHNS ON?"

"What?"

"Do you have your long Johns on?" Jim Irving asked his brother Jack.

"Sure. What do you think? Do you?"

The oldest of the three brothers pulled up a pantleg and displayed a length of winter underwear above his socks. Jack opened his shirt to reveal he was wearing a sweater underneath it in addition to his long johns.

They had spent the day with a reporter from *Maclean's* magazine who was trying to do what reporters had been trying to do for half a century or more: get to the core of the so-called Irving Empire.

At first they had said no to his request for an interview. It was the normal answer. They were not interested. They didn't have the time. But he was determined. He kept calling — one brother after the other. He wanted to get their side of the story. He wanted to be fair. Finally, he broke through. They agreed to see him.

They took him on a tour of some of the companies — the shipyard, the oil refinery, the pulp and paper mills. They took him aboard one of their ocean-going tankers and had lunch with him. They took him to the Irving Tank Farm overlooking the harbour and the bay, and the Irving Deepwater Terminal — and, to get the proper view, Arthur insisted they climb a ladder to the top of one of the tanks.

It was January. The temperature was −19, and the winds were high and bitterly cold. "I don't think he enjoyed that part of it," said Jack as Arthur entered the office and joined his brothers around a conference table. "Have you got your long johns on?" asked Jack.

Arthur looked perplexed. "No, why?"—at the same time throwing up his right leg and revealing an expanse of bare leg above his sock. "What's all this about long johns?"

Jim and Jack slapped the table and laughed. "You must have frozen out there today," said Jim.

"Are you wearing long johns?" Arthur asked.

"Sure," said Jim, "you don't think we're crazy enough to go out in that weather in summer clothes, do you?"

"Why didn't you tell me?"

"Why didn't you ask?" said Jack.

It was a meeting of three of the most powerful men in Canada, and it sounded more like a group of teenagers sitting around in a school locker room after some sporting event. The brothers Irving were relaxed, verbally horsing around at the end of another long day.

A day with a reporter was an unusual experience for the brothers, but this writer had pestered and they finally agreed. His name was John DeMont. He was from Halifax, a fellow Maritimer. He was bright, articulate, congenial. He'd made a good impression.

But, still, something bothered them. He hadn't asked many questions. He wrote very little down, used no tape recorder. He was a good conversationalist but he didn't seem to be after a lot of information. This led them to the uneasy conclusion that the story was already written and that he was looking only for an angle, perhaps for one or two facts to support some preconceived position. Was it to be another journalistic hit job? Had they been suckered? They didn't think so, or they didn't want to. He seemed straightforward enough, a decent young man. But why hadn't he asked more questions? Why didn't he write things down?

"He kept coming back to that article in *Forbes*," said Jim.

Arthur: "Well that's just a lot of crap and we told him so."

In 1988, a story in *Forbes* magazine had identified K.C. Irving as one of the richest men in the world. It said he was worth $8 billion, and that placed him in third position behind Japan's Yoshiaki Tsutsumi, $18.9 billion; and Taikichiro Mori, $18 billion.

This, the brothers thought, had become an obsession with DeMont. He'd tried to get confirmation from the three of them both together and individually. They said they didn't know — and they didn't — but this hadn't satisfied him. It did strengthen their suspicion that the story was already written, much of it from old clippings and probably much from unfriendly sources. Now, was he just looking for confirmation or denial of the $8 billion figure to give it some freshness?

They were going to see DeMont the next day, and they wished he'd get off that subject of the richest men in the world.

They found it embarrassing. They didn't flaunt or hoard their money. They poured it back into their businesses. They expanded. They bought new businesses, they modernized — and they resented it when articles speculated on the worth of the so-called Irving Empire.

"It's a lot of hogwash," said Jim, "and it isn't true."

"Well," said Arthur, "just tell him that. It isn't true. It's a lot of crap. That's it. Chapter closed."

Jack replied, "Yes ... but then he'll want to know what is true? Is it more or less?"

Finally, Jim: "We don't know and we don't care, and we don't spend any time worrying about it. We've got enough to do just running our businesses. Right?"

Arthur: "Right."

Jack: "Right."

And then, an afterthought from Arthur: "And if we don't know — and we don't — no one else does either. So let them speculate all they want to." The three brothers looked over the conference table at one another, paused, and then nodded. The meeting was over.

Now they were relaxed again. Then Jack said, "We should have had Dad give them his answer." They broke into laughter as they remembered how their father had handled the same question when he was being honoured by the Rotary Club in his boyhood home of Bouctouche the previous summer.

Asked by a reporter if the *Forbes* figure was correct, Kenneth Colin Irving, then eighty-nine, had replied by asking, "What figure?" When told the magazine had said he was worth $8 billion, he smiled an inscrutable smile and remarked, "Is that all?"

Then he walked away.

−30−

Art Irving's Dad

TWELVE YEARS had slipped away since that memorable night in Toronto when K.C. Irving was given national recognition and acclaim during his induction into the Canadian Business Hall of Fame. It was a night to remember — and, since he was in his eighty-first year, there were those who thought it might be his final public tribute.

But now, on November 20, 1991, Irving was being feted once again, for much the same reason — his lifetime contribution to the economic development of Atlantic Canada — and this time by an audience of business and political leaders. They turned out at the Saint John Trade and Convention Centre hoping to see and pay tribute to this legendary figure. As he neared his ninety-third birthday, he was to receive the Distinguished Service Award of the Atlantic Canada Plus Association, an organization dedicated to the cause of economic prosperity for Atlantic Canada.

For days there had been speculation as to whether he would be there. He no longer enjoyed robust health. Many did not expect him to show, yet there was a sense of disappointment when he didn't. But as the evening unfolded, disappointment was replaced by enthusiasm, excitement, and finally an almost euphoric feeling of goodwill and appreciation.

The crowd of more than five hundred had come from all corners of the four provinces. Tributes poured forth from federal and provincial politicians, from Derek Burney, Canada's ambassador to the United States, who, as a boy growing up in Northern Ontario, knew that the New Brunswicker had a reputation "as being as tough as they come." What Canada needed was "more people like Irving."

The mayor, the irrepressible Elsie Wayne, serving her ninth record-breaking year as the city's chief magistrate and soon to be elected for another three-year term, praised the Irvings for the businesses and employment they had created. An unabashed and unapologetic ham, she couldn't resist telling the audience about Arthur Irving's beautiful legs. How did she know? It didn't have anything to do with this night or the tribute to K.C. Irving, but the mayor told the story anyway.

It happened one night in a Bangor hotel, where she and her husband were staying on a return trip to Saint John. The fire alarm went off in the middle of the night and her husband shouted, "Get your slacks on, Elsie, we're getting out of here." They rushed to the lobby and the first person they met was Arthur Irving, who also had wasted no time in responding to the fire alarm. The mayor said she couldn't help admiring his plaid shirt. It was a beautiful shirt, she claimed, but that wasn't all that caught her eye — because Arthur hadn't taken the time to put on his pants. "So I can tell you that he has beautiful legs," she exclaimed to a delighted audience.

But now it was Arthur Irving's turn. Though a recent heart surgery patient, he bounded up from the audience to accept the trophy that honoured his father. For a moment it appeared that he was about to give a formal, thank-you-on-behalf-of-dad response. But almost immediately his thoughts, his feelings for his father came bubbling forth. It was a no-notes, no-preparation, strictly off-the-cuff speech of his life. It was also typical Arthur Irving: fractured delivery, banking, turning, shifting gears in mid-sentence, and all the time driving his points home with his own, personal staccato delivery, one thought pounding its way forward, pushing others aside, and then veering off in a new direction.

What was it like to work with K.C. Irving, to be a son of K.C. Irving? It was, said Arthur, like being in the stands of a great sporting event. There was excitement every day. Every day there was something new. His father was a fighter, a competitor, a winner.

"Every day was a new game. The score was three to two. We were two and the other guy was three. We had about ten seconds to play and we had to win. He got a big charge out of being successful."

And, yes, K.C. Irving was tough. It was a tough world, "and he was as tough as they come. I would put him up against any businessman in the world." But there was another side to K.C. Irving. He was a man of his word. He would make huge deals on a handshake. His word was his bond.

He was a man who could be humble. In the home he was always polite. He never used bad language. He appreciated the efforts of loyal employees. If the senior Irving had been present, he would have said that anything that had been achieved could not have been done without "all the good and faithful employees" in the Irving organization. He was not present, said Arthur, because he had had a "bad spell" and had just been released after spending two weeks in hospital. But he had talked to his father by phone just before dinner and his father had told him three times to "make sure you thank everyone."

It had been an unusual speech, a shifting and darting talk in which a son had given the audience a fleeting glimpse of a remarkable man, but more importantly it was a penetrating, even naked view of the warmth, affection, and love of the Irving sons for their father. And then, just as it seemed that everything had been said, there was one final point, and it was made in a moving and touching way: "He's been a great father," Arthur said. "A great friend."

−30−

Epilogue

THE THREE BROTHERS stand near the foot of the casket, greeting mourners, chatting with friends. As an old associate of their father's approaches Arthur steps forward to give him a smiling, gracious welcome. The man had known Arthur's father for, what, thirty or forty years? Yes, closer to forty. A long time. Small talk follows, the type common at funeral homes. The man had not seen K.C. in recent months and it is a troubling, emotional experience.

The once-robust frame of the man who led and dominated more than a half-century of industrial development in New Brunswick seems small, too frail in death. Eye glasses are perched on his aquiline nose, and the visitor wonders if it was unanimous or perhaps a two-to-one vote that put them there. Then he remembers there would have been four votes: K.C.'s wife Winnifred, Jim, Arthur, Jack. No vote would have been necessary for what next catches his eye. K.C. is wearing his blue blazer, that proud uniform of old age with its First World War Royal Flying Corps crest. Appropriate, he thinks. The Old Warrior is going to his grave with at least a vestige of a fighter's regalia. Soon he will join his first wife Harriet in Christ Church Presbyterian Cemetery in Warwick, Bermuda. It is a moment of sadness, a realization that this giant of New Brunswick's twentieth century is gone.

Arthur breaks the silence: "He looks good, doesn't he?" The man chokes up. He can't speak. The brothers back off, leave him for a moment to compose himself. It is a scene that is repeated over and over. The city mourns. The province mourns. In his memorial service, Rev. Philip Lee will say, "All New Brunswick weeps today." It is true. A sense of sadness and loss has gripped the province.

K.C. had come from Bermuda to spend the Christmas season with family, back to the home of his heart, to the penthouse atop the new Irving Building in the centre of Saint John. The address was 300 Union Street, the very site where he had established his first Ford dealership sixty-seven years earlier.

Now a freeman of the city that had seemed too cold and forbidding those many years ago, he was where he wanted to be, in a place of memories and vast accomplishments. In the days ahead he would visit with his sons and their families, see grandchildren and great-grandchildren. He was ninety-three and there was growing concern about his health, about a weakening heart. The sons visited him regularly and he was accompanied everywhere by Winnifred. The Irving company doctor kept an anxious eye on his activities.

Irving businesses were as he would want them to be: under the absolute control of his sons and their children. Control met his own personal definition of what majority ownership should be: 100 per cent. Partners of convenience and necessity in the oil refinery, the oil company, the pulp and tissue mills had been bought out and were gone. Everything was in order. His work was done. From now on, it would be up to The Boys.

It was here, then, in Saint John, at 300 Union Street, where so much of it had started, that it came to an end. Death occurred early Sunday, December 13, 1992, four months short of his ninety-fourth birthday. On Monday morning the *Telegraph-Journal*, that newspaper he believed had given him more than his share of black ink so the editors could "keep their skirts clean," used eight pages of words and pictures to trace his life from a lively, rambunctious boyhood to international success, power, and recognition.

Public and private tributes would support that view. Many had a common thread: it was the end of an era and Irving's accomplishments were monumental. Liberal leader Jean Chrétien attended the funeral, as did New Brunswick Premier

Frank McKenna and members of his cabinet. Prime Minister Mulroney, busy in Ottawa honouring Toronto's World Series Champion Blue Jays, issued a public tribute and called members of the family to express his regrets. Messages of sympathy poured in, from people of power, little people, employees, and strangers.

Harrison McCain, head of New Brunswick's internationally renowned food-processing company, recalled his early training with the Irvings in the 1950s and the influence Irving had on his life and the lives of others. To the pleasure of the family, he remembered a man few people knew, a relaxed, fun-loving Irving. "He was good fun to be with, a great storyteller — with plenty of stories to tell." R. Whidden Ganong, eighty-six-year-old patriarch of the New Brunswick candy-making family, had known Irving since the 1920s when they had business operations on opposite sides of a street in Saint John. He recalled asking Irving for advice occasionally and remembered one of Irving's rules of business: "Always be honest in what you do." It was, said Ganong, good advice.

Among those at the memorial service from Irving's hometown of Bouctouche was Jean-Paul Robichaud. He had worked for the Irvings for twenty years and remembered K.C. with fondness and awe. The previous summer he had been asked to trim trees in front of Irving's house at Bouctouche so K.C. could sit in the window and see activity at a nearby Irving service station. "He was ninety-three and he wanted to see how many cars were going in to buy gas!"

Old adversaries were among those who commended Irving's lifetime of accomplishments. Retired senator Charles McElman, one of the most persistent critics of Irving's media ownership in the 1960s and '70s, had used bitter words about that ownership but never about Irving himself. His assessment now of Irving's achievements was unequivocal: "Of all the contacts I've had over the years in public affairs and otherwise, nationally and internationally, he is the one person I've known whom I would say was possessed of absolute genius, in business and finance. He made money work for him, he didn't work for money. That resounded to the benefit of New Brunswick." McElman made other points that could have been taken direct from the Irving bible on business: all benefits were poured back into New Brunswick, and he believed that if the head office was in New Brunswick, decisions would be made in New Brunswick and profits retained in the province.

Senator Louis Robichaud, the former New Brunswick premier who had a falling out with Irving in the 1960s, said he still admired the man. "I have admired K.C. Irving ever since I was a kid growing up in Kent County, and that admiration has never ceased in my life. We had our ups and downs but I never lost my admiration for his courage and determination." But Robichaud also acknowledged that their personal rift had never healed. Of their differences, he said Irving "had a memory like an elephant."

Long-time New Brunswick politician Gerry Merrithew, then federal minister of veterans' affairs and previously minister of forestry, had special praise for Irving's reforestation program. He also recalled that the Saint John newsprint mill "was going nowhere when the Irvings took it over in 1982" and "the shipyard was a collapsing company" when it was acquired. "The Irvings never took a cent out of it. They poured it back in to make it one of the most modern shipyards in the world."

A more personal anecdote came from Fredericton Member of Parliament Bud Bird. As a young man living in Saint John, he had become stuck in a snowbank. A stranger stopped, took him to a nearby Irving service station, and told the attendant to give him good service and help him out of the jam he was in. It was only after the man left that the service station worker told him his Good Samaritan was K.C. Irving.

Then there was the message penned by Eddie Sheehan, that tough-minded, straight-talking engineer from Boston who had lived through those classic confrontations with Irving during construction projects at the Irving Pulp and Paper mill in Saint John. Seventy-nine, long retired, and living in Plymouth, Massachusetts, he sent this note to the sons: "Your Dad went through life providing richly for others, leaving footprints that will be indelible forever."

The Reverend Philip Lee was one of those with a special Irving story, and he told it during the memorial service. It involved plans for another Irving family funeral at which an overflow crowd was anticipated: "Mr. Irving and, I believe, all three sons were busy arranging things downstairs in our hall. He wanted tables set up and flowers arranged so that the people down there would not feel left out of the worship service. Mr. Irving was close to eighty at the time and I was a much younger man. I started to move one of our folding tables when he said, 'Reverend Lee, don't move that table. My sons and I are used to this kind of work.' Now, maybe he didn't trust a preacher with that kind of work, but whatever his motive—his courtesy and modesty left me speechless."

That sermon, paradoxically, was preached in the Presbyterian Church of St. John and St. Stephen, the church whose construction Irving had so staunchly and stubbornly opposed in the 1960s. The property was too cramped, he maintained, the church itself too small, and there was no parking space. It was, he insisted, a terrible location for the church, so bad a choice that he would not give a cent to the building fund. Instead, as a face-saving measure for himself and probably more particularly for his church-going wife, he paid the minister's salary for several years.

Now, at his own funeral, overflow crowds watched the service on closed-circuit television in the church basement and on giant screens set up in a nearby school auditorium and gymnasium. They arrived by limousine, taxis, public transportation, and on foot after a worried police chief made a city-wide appeal through the media: "Leave your cars at home," he pleaded. "There is no parking at the church."

Kenneth Colin Irving, that remarkable huckleberry from Bouctouche, New Brunswick—stubborn, obstinate, and so often right—had made his point, this time virtually from the grave.

—30—

One of a Kind

‒ ‒ ‒ ‒ ‒ ‒ ‒
‒ ‒ ‒ ‒ ‒
‒

HE WAS BORN just before the turn of the century in the small coastal community of Bouctouche in eastern New Brunswick. He lived for 93 years and changed forever the face of his native province.

He was a man of dogged determination. Stubborn. At times obstinately stubborn, yet he was also a man of vision, a builder and a dreamer who made his dreams come true.

For much of his life he was a loner, determined to control his own destiny. He took chances and would not be encumbered, delayed or held back by those less bold, less venturesome. From the very beginning, from his earliest days in business in Bouctouche, he was a fighter; he didn't know how to back off or back down.

He was quiet, reserved, at times shy. He was instinctively and honestly courteous. It was not an act. That was his way. That was how he grew up in a home where discipline and courtesy were the order of the day. He had a lively sense of humour and a laugh that brought a sparkle to his eyes.

Those same eyes could turn to ice when he was crossed or felt someone had gone back on a deal. It was a tough world and he was as tough as they come, but not mean. He knew the difference.

He took old, tired businesses and made them whole again, nursed them back to health, built on them, branched out, invested earnings in new ventures. He believed in New Brunswick and Canada with a passion matched by few.

He was suspicious of those who came from away, or outsiders who, he believed, would exploit New Brunswick, use her resources and finally leave the province and her people the poorer. He believed in reinvesting profits so that businesses were always growing, always expanding, always exploring new horizons. It was his creed, the bible of his business philosophy.

He defied and confounded the experts.

The experts said a rundown pulp mill in Saint John could not be operated economically. They were so sure they advised the banks not to lend him money. He got the money anyway, bought the mill and ran it seven days a week, proving the experts wrong. His forest operations supplied the mill and soon there were sawmills, a newsprint mill, a tissue mill and a packaging plant. Fleets of trucks carried products around New Brunswick, throughout the Atlantic provinces, across Canada and into the United States. And so it was in the business and dozens of others.

One of his lifelong ambitions was to build an oil refinery. That refinery was built and became the largest in Canada. He located it in Saint John, not because that was the most appropriate marketing centre for it, but because Saint John was his home.

Saint John's aging drydock was acquired and rebuilt into a world-class shipyard that would construct ships for his companies, then for others, even for his competitors. Finally it would win the greatest shipbuilding contract in Canadian history.

The experts said he couldn't grow trees. They said he didn't have the professional knowledge. He was going about it the wrong way. He grew them anyway, by the thousands, then by the millions and, eventually, by the hundreds of millions. Others followed his example and started reforestation programs of their own. His onetime critics honoured him, said he had been right all along. He thanked them and went on to new challenges.

He worked long hours seven days a week. From his employees he expected a day's work for a day's pay. He had run-ins with labour, but he created thousands upon thousands of jobs. He jump-started and fuelled the economy of New Brunswick as no one else had ever done. He made the wheels turn.

In everything he did, in every venture, he held the reins tightly. He was in charge. He was old school. He could, it seemed, do anything and everything better than those who worked for him. He delegated sparingly, and it was believed he would never let go.

But then one day, with little or no warning, his sons were in charge. Soon their children were active as apprentices, then as managers and bosses. The business continued to expand around the Atlantic provinces, into Quebec, into the United States, and beyond.

He had always believed in free trade and he had lived to see it happen — to see the vast markets to the south open up for the bold of heart. He would not see the fruits of that great experiment, but his children would, and their children's children. Of that he was convinced.

His good works will live long after him. They will benefit countless thousands of New Brunswickers who will have access to better lives because of the doors he opened and the opportunities he created — because of the dreams and the enterprise of one man.

There are those, presumably, who will say he did only what someone else would have done if he had not been here. They are wrong. He was mortal but he was also special. Different. Unique. One of a kind. K.C. Irving, dead at 93. He was a builder.

−30−

THE EARLY YEARS

A Man with "The Weakness"

– – – – – – –
– – – – –
–

IT WAS PAY DAY and the woman was waiting for her husband to come home. There had not been a pay day in that house for months. Maybe a year or more. In fact, it was hard to remember when her husband had last worked. She knew he was lucky now to have anything because this was the time of the Great Depression.

There was little work even for the skilled and reliable. Her husband, she knew, was neither. There was nothing special about him or his skills. As well, he had "the weakness." The weakness for drink.

But now, and at least for the moment, there was hope. At the end of the day he would have money in his pocket for the first time in months. But that was also reason for worry. That was why she couldn't settle down, why she went every few minutes to look anxiously out the front window. The boy, not yet ten but worldly beyond his years, watched all this with growing anxiety. He sensed that things were not going to work out. He, too, knew about his father's weakness.

Dan Morrissey had agreed to give the man another chance as a cook in his uptown restaurant. He had worked before for Morrissey and had let him down, but Dan Morrissey was a kindly man. Something of an optimist. He had a family himself and he knew how much a job meant in those days. So now, probably against his better judgment, he had gone out on the limb once again because he knew the family, and the man's wife had promised that her husband would behave. He had learned his lesson. He would be on the job every day. He would stay off the bottle. He had promised his wife and then he made the same promise to Dan Morrissey. He was going to make a go of it this time. He was not going to let anyone down.

Today, all that good resolve would be tested. It was the end of the week. Pay day. This was the setting as the boy sat quietly and watched his mother wait and suffer. He knew she was praying. There was nothing else she could do, so she prayed and waited far into the night. There was no reason for her to go to bed. Sleep was out of the question.

The boy went to bed but he could not sleep either. He heard his mother moving about the house. Heard her crying, and he felt helpless because there was nothing he could do to help her.

Finally, sometime after midnight, they heard the voice of a man singing. In truth, it was not singing. The man couldn't carry a tune. It was more like shouting. Like a drunken man shouting a tuneless song in the night. The mother and the boy now knew what they had known all along.

The voice became less strident as it neared the house and stopped abruptly as the man came through the door. Now there was nothing to sing about. Nothing to talk about. Nothing to discuss. Nothing to be interrogated about. Nothing he would answer for. He'd had a drink or two, and what about it? So he told his wife to shut up when she asked where he had been and if he had any money left.

"Shut up," he said. "Stop nagging. Shut your goddamn mouth."

Then he went to bed and slept in the next morning because he was tired and hung over. After that it didn't make any difference. There was no reason to get up. Nothing to do. No place to go. No job to go to.

"The weakness" had won another round.

A Mother's Love

_ _ _ _ _ _ _
_ _ _ _ _
_

HER COAT WAS THREADBARE. Her hair was combed straight. She had an attractive face but her eyes would tell you she was weary, that she was tired and life was difficult. She was in her early thirties but looked older. On this day, in the Depression, in 1932, she had walked several miles to a hospital on the outskirts of the city to see her son. He was nine years old. He had TB.

Tuberculosis was the scourge of the time. She had seen it run through entire families. She had watched young men and women cut down in what should have been the prime of their lives.

Brothers and sisters of her husband had been victims. She had watched them die. Neighbours and friends also had been stricken. She and her husband came from a working-class neighbourhood where people knew they were fortunate to have a job. Any job. Young school dropouts, barely in their teens, waited anxiously for jobs to open up at the Cotton Mill. Yet for many the mill and tuberculosis would be nothing more than a ticket to an early grave. Now, this mother who had seen so much sadness, sickness, and death had to live every day with the knowledge that the scourge was visiting the next generation of her family.

But this was her son's birthday and somehow she would put on a bright face, if only for this one special day. She had taken a gift to her son and watched anxiously for his reaction. It was a flint gun, shaped like a revolver, and when he pulled the trigger it made a scratching sound and sparks came out of the barrel. But, most important of all, he was pleased with it. She could see that and her eyes lit up as she shared his moment of happiness.

The play gun was small and flimsy, soon to run out of flint and fire. It might have cost twenty-five or fifty cents. Fifty cents? No, probably not. That would have fed the family for two days. Maybe longer. The mother could buy stale bread for five cents a loaf. She could go to a corner grocery store and have a pint bottle filled with molasses for a few cents. People knew how to stretch their meagre resources in those days. Sometimes, the boy would learn later, workers at the bakery would give her bread even if she didn't have any money. She didn't have to tell them she was hungry or that her family was in need. Everyone, it seemed, was hungry in those days.

So how could she afford to buy even a five-and-dime flint gun? The boy didn't think those thoughts on that day. It didn't matter to him. He pulled the trigger and saw fire leap from the gun. "Bang," he said. "Bang, bang." He shot the boy in the next bed. Don't fool around with Tom Mix, pardner! Or whoever was the reigning cowboy hero of the day. Years later, many years later, the boy would remember that day. He would remember it with a tear just a blink away as he thought of all the sacrifices his mother had endured for him and other members of the family. And, invariably, his thoughts would return to that little flint gun.

In old age he would wonder about the story behind that birthday present. He would remember that it did not come in fancy wrapping. There was no package held together with a colourful ribbon. There was no birthday card. Just a scratchy flint gun, and he would try to imagine how his mother could have managed even that.

Perhaps she had gone to Joe Gilbert's Second Hand Store and Pawn Shop on Dock Street. She would have told Gilbert she needed a present for her boy who was in hospital. She would pay for it later. When she had some money.

It would not have been the first trip to Joe Gilbert's to sell or pawn to buy something, nor would it have been unusual for Joe Gilbert to find a way to help. This was the Depression. He was a pawn-shop dealer in business on the outer edge of society but he also had a heart. People helped people when they could.

Sometimes their kindness would be repaid. Other times there was no money to pay them. That's the way it was in the 1930s.

But one thing was certain on that day. No matter where it came from or how she got it, the boy's mother had to have a present for her nine-year-old son. The boy with TB. Because she loved him.

The boy would spend six months in hospital, gain twenty-five pounds, and enjoy good health for the rest of his days. The mother would live into her nineties and experience a mother's ultimate joy of seeing a once-sickly boy healthy and well on his way to a long and productive life.

−30−

The Golden Rule

– – – – – – –
– – – – –
–

"WHY ARE YOU hanging around here?" the man wanted to know.

"I'm waiting for me brother," the boy replied.

"Waiting for me brother," the man mocked. "Well, wait across the street."

The man was principal of the school attended by the boy's older brother. The school was on a street corner and the principal was exercising his authority, real or imagined, to order people about even if they were on a public street. Or perhaps he reserved this treatment just for young boys who came from poor families and didn't speak the language very well.

No matter. The man, towering over the boy, had all the authority he needed. In fact, he was a symbol of power and authority. He stood ramrod straight, had hawk-like features, hair slicked back, and looked like he should have been a sergeant major. If only there had been a war. In short, his order was not debatable.

So the boy went quietly to the other side of the street, where he waited for his older brother. Then, together, they would go to the newspaper office on Canterbury Street and down Church Street to the side entrance, where they would wait with other youngsters for the afternoon papers. They were newsboys trying to make a few cents in the Depression years. One day both would be newspapermen, but that was still years away.

The school principal? He was well known in those days back in the 1930s, and he would become prominent and well respected in the future, eventually holding important positions in the province's education system.

The two newsboys also achieved a measure of success, and in later years the boy who was "waiting for me brother" would remember the streetcorner encounter with a degree of amusement, but also as a valuable lesson — a lesson in how not to treat those less fortunate. It was something about the Golden Rule, and then there was that other old saying about being nice to people on the way up because....

−30−

God, They Believed, Would Understand

‒ ‒ ‒ ‒ ‒ ‒ ‒
‒ ‒ ‒ ‒ ‒
‒

FIVE CENTS.

Each boy had five cents.

For Sunday church collection.

But they spent it on candy.

Then they went upstairs and sat in the balcony of the church.

Alone.

Where they munched furtively and guiltily on their candy. One small piece at a time.

If they thought anyone was looking at them, or that anyone suspected what they were up to—and especially if the preacher, the Rev. Dr. S.S. Poole, gave them the eye—they would stop chewing and just suck on the candy.

They knew it was wrong. Wrong to spend the collection money on candy, and wrong to eat it in church. But it tasted good just the same.

The church deacons, the men who passed the collection plates, never bothered to go upstairs where the boys were sitting alone. They knew them. They knew they didn't have any money. They were poor boys from a poor neighbourhood. At Christmas they got boxes of food from the church and the Empty Stocking Fund. They were Mary Costello's boys and their father didn't work. Or if he worked he drank. He wasn't about to give them money for the church.

But the boys had their own money. They made it selling newspapers. They gave most of it to their mother, and on Sunday she would give each of them five cents for church collection. It was money, she told them, that the church would send to missionaries who were trying to feed the starving in India or China, or somewhere in some foreign country.

It was good training for the boys. No matter how little they had, there was always someone with less. That's what their mother told them. They believed her, and usually the money would go right where it was supposed to go—first into the collection plate and then, presumably, on to the missionaries. For the starving children of the world.

But sometimes the temptation was too great, and when it was they would buy candy and sit in the church balcony.

Their mother didn't know. Neither did anyone else. Only the boys, and possibly the preacher who, come to think of it, was pretty perceptive.

Then, of course, there was God, but they figured He wouldn't mind.

It was only five cents. Five cents each.

That bought a lot of candy in the Depression Years.

A whole bagfull each. Which they ate.

–30–

Afternoon Tea

_ _ _ _ _ _ _
_ _ _ _ _
_

THE MAN'S NAME WAS COLLIE.

But the boy could never remember the name of the woman. The man's wife. There were two daughters. At the time he thought they were pretty. Maybe they were. They were young, about his age, nine or ten.

The mother, whose name the boy could not remember, was a long-time friend of his mother's, and when Collie and his family were out for a Sunday walk they would stop by for a visit, and his mother would make some tea and sometimes there would be something small to eat.

At first and for a time they visited only occasionally. Then it became a Sunday afternoon ritual. Every Sunday. Soon, the visits became strained and tense. The families would sit in the kitchen, but now there seemed to be less to talk about, and the boy's mother knew that at the very least she was expected to offer her visitors a cup of tea. But this was the Depression, when every cent counted. Now, instead of being happy to see her friends, she was uncomfortable and embarrassed. The boy could sense the change, but Collie and his family couldn't. Or maybe they just didn't care.

In later years the boy remembered that he had never visited their home. He didn't even know where they lived. His mother didn't visit them either. She would say her social days, if there ever had been any, were behind her. It was the Depression. People tried to survive. They didn't socialize. Except for Collie and his wife. And the two pretty daughters.

Then one Sunday the boy's mother said if Collie and his family came that day she wasn't going to answer the door. They would pretend they were not home.

"I can't feed them anymore," she said.

It wasn't much. Often little more than a cup of tea, but it was food off her table. Out of the mouths of her own family. So she warned her family to be quiet that afternoon, and when there was a knock no one said anything.

The knocking grew louder, and then there was a pause and a form appeared at the window. Collie was trying to see if anyone was at home. But there were no lights on in the house and there was nothing he could see through the curtains.

Soon the knocking resumed. Louder and louder, but no one answered. No one said anything.

Then—and this time it was not a knock but a hard kick, and the door all but shuddered. And the man said, loud enough for everyone to hear, "goddammit."

He knew people were in the house. Where would they go? It was the Depression. So he gave one final, defiant kick. That was his message. That was his goodbye. Then the family walked away, never to return. Collie and his wife and the two pretty daughters.

The boy's mother shook her head sadly and cried a little that afternoon. She would miss them, especially Collie's wife, her girlhood friend.

But the boy wouldn't miss them at all because he didn't think Collie should have peeked in the window and kicked the door like that. He didn't like the swearing either. Finally, in later years when he occasionally saw the two daughters somewhere in the city, he realized they weren't very pretty after all.

—30—

The Price of Honesty

—————
————
—

SIXTY-FIVE AND MORE years later, in old age, he would remember that day in the early 1930s. He would remember the tantalizing smell of caramel popcorn and the sight of it being stirred and popped in a large metal container and then covered with a dark golden syrup. He could still see the bulging, full-to-the-brim white bags that were placed in the window of a small Charlotte Street store in the centre of the city.

He would remember that virtually everything in the store was white. Everything but the caramel-covered popcorn. It cost five cents a bag, or ten cents for a larger bag that would have lasted longer than the boy could even imagine.

But he didn't have ten cents. He didn't have five cents. It was the Depression. People didn't have money, and those who did—at least, those among the people he knew—would not have squandered it on popcorn.

Unless they happened to be a ten-year-old boy who stood all but transfixed within sight and smell of what he knew had to be the most luscious, delicious candied popcorn in the whole world. Something so near, yet completely beyond his reach. It was on the other side of a store window but it might just as well have been on the other side of the world. So the boy stood with his face pressed against the window, and the warm aroma filtered out and all but saturated his very being. But he had no money. It was all wishful thinking.

Then, just as he was about to leave, because there was no reason to remain and torture himself any longer, a wagon pulled out of the alley beside the store. A man in rough clothing held the reins to guide the horse that pulled one of the low-slung slovens that were common in Saint John at that time. It was obvious that the man was a garbage collector but he also had collected what could only be several bags of popcorn. They had been separated from the trash and neatly stacked on top of a large wooden box at the front of the wagon. There had to be twenty or more bags.

And then the man spotted the boy.

"Here, kid," he said, "want a bag?"

The boy hesitated.

"It's okay," the man said. "It just isn't fresh."

He held out a white paper bag.

Full of popcorn.

But still the boy hesitated.

Was it honest, he wondered? Was it all right? Should the man be giving away popcorn? Wasn't he supposed to take it somewhere? Did he even own it? A minute earlier the boy had desperately wanted even the smallest taste of that coffee-coloured delicacy, but now he wasn't sure. He wondered what his mother would say. She had taught him that, at all costs, no matter what, he had to be honest.

"Here, catch," said the man, about to toss a bag to the boy.

"No. No, thank you," the boy said.

Then he wished he hadn't.

But he had. The words just popped out.

And once they had he knew immediately it would have been all right. He knew it wasn't stealing. He knew he could have taken that bag of popcorn and it would have tasted just as good as if it had been fresh. But now it was too late.

The man shrugged, flicked the reins on the back of the horse.

And drove off.

The Man from the Church

– – – – – – –
– – – – –
–

SOMEONE WAS KNOCKING on the door. Loudly. Impatiently. "Is anyone home?" a man's voice called out. "Is anyone in there?"

But no one answered. It might have been the landlord coming for rent money that no one had. Perhaps the truant officer looking for boys who should have been in school. Or someone from the hydro to turn off the electricity. A knock on the door, the family knew from experience, was more likely to be bad news than good in those grim Depression Years.

As the knocking and the voice grew louder, the boy recognized the voice. It was a man from the church, a man who taught Sunday school and supervised a boys' group known as Trail Rangers.

It was, the boy realized, the man who delivered the Empty Stocking Fund Christmas packages to poor families. It was something he did every year.

"It's the Empty Stocking Fund," he said to his mother. It's the man from church. From Sunday school."

The mother nodded, breathed a tired sigh, and opened the door.

It was, as the boy had said, the man from the church, but he was not alone. He was accompanied by several boys, youngsters the boy's own age, the boys he played basketball with when he went to Trail Rangers. They were, in his mind, the rich kids from the church.

There were four or five of them. Perhaps six. Together with the man, they crowded into what must have been a strange room for them, barren of furniture, dingy, and cold by any standards they would have known.

They carried a box of food and small presents, which they placed on the floor just inside the door. One of them said "Hi" to the boy.

Embarrassed, he nodded and turned away.

The man, he remembered—and he would always remember—was brusque and businesslike. He was polite, in his own way, but there was no warmth in his voice. That, too, the boy would remember. The man told the boy's mother the packages were from the Empty Stocking Fund, the turkey and other gifts of food from the church. He said he hoped she would have a Merry Christmas.

She said thank you. She meant it. The gifts, the turkey, the food, meant everything to her. The difference between a Christmas and no Christmas. She was grateful. She wished the man and the boys a Merry Christmas.

Then, as if on cue, the visitors shouted Merry Christmas, but the boy didn't reply.

A moment later they were gone, and the boy was relieved that it was over. He helped his mother unpack the box but he didn't say anything to her about how he felt, and he told himself he didn't care if they knew he was poor. But he did.

And when he next went to Trail Rangers and basketball practice, he scored more baskets than any of them and in a way that made up for it. For the embarrassment. The humiliation.

But he never forgot.

Later, much later in life, he wondered how a man from the church could be so insensitive. Why did he have to bring all those boys to see where and how he lived in the Depression? It was something that bothered him for a long time.

The Swimming Champion

— — — — — — —
— — — — —
—

MANY YEARS LATER, half a century and more later, in old age, he would think of that magical summer when a young boy lived in a fantasy world and dreamed of the great achievements and conquests that would be his in the future. He didn't know it then but they were the dreams of young boys the world over. They were part of growing up, part of the fantasy world that was theirs to live, theirs to enjoy and conquer.

One day, he would be a world swimming champion. Perhaps he would become a professional golfer or, if he wished, basketball might be his career. He would have to decide that later but it was only a matter of time and choice. He was fourteen, the year was 1937, and life was wonderful.

Dreams. They shut out the reality of the grim world of the Depression. They kindled the spirit of the young while adults were left to struggle and worry, driven down and beaten into submission by the harshness and the unfairness of the times.

There were other dreams but they too were exclusively for the young—dreams, for instance, of the most beautiful girl in the village. The old man remembered her well. Sixty years later he remembered the long flaxen hair, sometimes worn in braids, sometimes combed out to shoulder length. He remembered her face and lips, her figure, the clothes she wore, the way she smiled.

The boy spent much of that summer around the Renforth Wharf, on the beach, and in the water of the Kennebecasis River. He was in training. In the warm cocoon of that summer's fantasy world, he was in training for the next Olympics — and, more immediately, the Rothesay Yacht Club Regatta.

She, too, was often at the beach, on the wharf, or in the clubhouse that was on the river's edge, a popular gathering place for young people of the community. He remembered the white shorts she wore that summer and how sometimes she would be in a bathing suit. She was there watching him as he swam back and forth along the shoreline or as he practised diving from the makeshift board at the end of the wharf. It was only natural, he thought, that she and others would watch him. He could swim better and faster than just about anyone in the village. He could do the crawl. The Australian crawl. It was his specialty. One day he would be as fast as Johnny Weissmuller, the Olympic swimming champion of the 1920s who later played Tarzan in the movies. Tarzan. Maybe he would be the next Tarzan. When he grew up. When he put on more weight. When he came home a hero from the Olympics.

A dream world? Of course, but also perfectly normal for a fourteen-year-old who had already won swimming and diving championships at the YMCA, at Pamdenac, and Lily Lake. So the boy practised harder than ever. He set higher goals, and there was a new incentive. He knew, or was almost certain, that she would be at the Rothesay Regatta — she and hundreds of others, because everyone went to regattas in those days. It was the thing to do, one of the highlights of the summer. Then, on that day, he would be ready. He would win all the events. Every one of them. He would be the champion. He would be her hero.

Reality, of course, was something else. His world was far removed from that of the most beautiful girl in the village. In truth, they were not a couple, not even close friends. Their only contact was in groups at the clubhouse. Still, years later, he thought that something could have been possible, there was chemistry between them that might have been ignited even at that early age if only . . . .

But the divide was great. She lived in a mansion-like home at the top of Renforth with a magnificent view of the Kennebecasis River. She was part of a family of wealth and influence. He, the boy, was living in a small camp that somehow, miraculously, his mother had rented for the summer. His older brother was the real breadwinner in their home, but there was not much he could do with his wages as a junior clerk at MRAs, the huge department store that was the centre of the retail business in Saint John. The boy made a few dollars as a caddie at the nearby golf course. The father came and went as he wished. Sometimes he had money for his wife, but often he didn't. She managed, as she always had, with what she had and by her wits. The family got by, but just barely.

Yet for the boy it had been a wonderful summer. He played golf with other caddies at daybreak before members arrived at the course. He learned to play tennis with a borrowed racquet. He won his swimming and diving championships at the Rothesay Regatta, and she was there with other supporters from Renforth to cheer him on. But that was all. That was where the dreams and the fantasy ended.

Now it was time for reality. Time for the most idyllic of all summers to end. In fact, in mere minutes it would be over forever as the boy and his mother waited for the bus that would take them back to the city.

But, as fate would have it, there was one more memory of that summer — a bittersweet memory — that the boy would take with him. Because, as he boarded the bus, there she was — sitting in the second row, returning from her day at school in Rothesay. Their eyes met, and as they were about to speak someone, undoubtedly one of her girlfriends, said in a stage whisper loud enough for everyone to hear: "There's your boyfriend."

There's your boyfriend! She might just as well have shouted it. Everyone on the bus was looking at him. School children and adults stared at him because this was a time before school buses, when students travelled by regular bus. The boy knew his face was a flaming red and not only because of what had been said. There was another reason for his embarrassment.

He looked straight ahead as he walked down the aisle to take a seat at the window and wait for his mother. He didn't know if the girl, the most beautiful girl in the village, had turned to watch him or not. He didn't want to know. It was too humiliating because of the hole in the heel of one of his stockings. His right stocking. He was wearing short pants and there was no way that hole could be hidden. No way she could have missed it. He was afraid that was the way she would remember him.

Soon, mercifully soon, only a few hundred yards down the road, the bus came to a stop. The door opened and she got off. But she never looked back. Her friends, giggling and whispering, got off with her. Then, as they did in those days, they stood by the side of the road until the bus moved off — and just as it started she looked up, smiled, and gave a little flutter with her hand. Just a flutter with her right hand that was on top of the books she was carrying. Not a real wave. But a wave nevertheless.

A small gesture, but it was remarkable what that smile and a fluttering wave meant to the boy. Suddenly he felt good all over, but only for a second, because now it was too late to wave back, and he could have kicked himself for that. He would remember her and he would remember that summer. But he would not see her again. He didn't know what became of her. They lived in different worlds.

But sometimes in old age when there was nothing more pressing to do, he would think back, as old people do, to his childhood and the girl with the flaxen hair. On those occasions, when the magic of that summer was with him once again, if only briefly and only in his memory, he would wonder what became of her and whether she would even remember that small boy, the swimming and diving champion. The boy with the hole in his stocking.

–30–

No One Is Hungry — Only the Poor People

———————
—————
—

THEY WOULD STAND OUTSIDE the front office of the old newspaper building on Canterbury Street, sometimes in the bitter cold of December, and it was not difficult to detect the sadness and despair in their eyes.

Sometimes they would come right up to the door of the office before turning away to walk back to the corner of Church and Canterbury Streets. There they would stand and think and breathe deeply before returning to enter the office. Other times they would just keep walking, perhaps never to return.

Some of those people were proud. Some didn't care, their spirit long since broken. Others were down on their luck, waiting and hoping for better days. They all had one thing in common: they were mothers and their children were facing a bleak Christmas.

They were Empty Stocking Fund mothers.

That was their only hope. The Empty Stocking Fund — the difference between an empty Christmas and some small measure of happiness for a child at home.

Those were the Depression Years. You had to live through those times to understand that it took a certain type of courage to walk through the front doors of that imposing brick building on Canterbury Street, to walk up to the front desk and ask for information about the Empty Stocking Fund.

But those days are gone. No one is hungry now.

Meanwhile, back in those grim days, a young Hugh Trueman would sit in the cramped broadcasting studio of radio station CHSJ and talk into a microphone for hours without interruption. He would sit in his shirtsleeves, his collar unbuttoned and his tie pulled down, his jacket discarded.

Hugh Trueman was Uncle Bill, and it was Uncle Bill and his Junior Radio Stars who started the tradition of a Christmas broadcast in Saint John.

Jene Wood began on that program, as did Clarence and Roger Fleiger; little David Longmire and Ting Walton, Audrie Milton, Norma MacMurray, and how many hundreds more?

But it was Uncle Bill's program. He was the kingpin. The program had started modestly enough away back in 1936, but it grew and grew and grew. And no matter how big it got, Hugh Trueman would carry it all in a frenzy of mass confusion. He stayed on the air. He read the pledges, interviewed the children, pleaded for more money, and conducted his races against the clock.

"Can we raise five hundred dollars by five o'clock?"

"Yes, we can do it, Uncle Bill," his Junior Radio Stars would scream.

And do it they would.

And there was never anything quite like it. It was Uncle Bill's tribute to Christmas. Without him there would be no radio program, no Christmas fund. No Christmas.

And then he was gone — gone from the station and soon off to Toronto for a new and successful career in broadcasting and advertising.

Yet the program continued. The Depression was but a memory, the war had come and gone, and while the Empty Stocking Fund remained, times had changed. No one in Saint John was really in need. No one was hungry.

But the spirit of Christmas prevailed, and for seventeen years Jene Wood charmed her way into the hearts of Saint John as she took over where Uncle Bill had left off.

She was energetic. She was vivacious, an actress, a singer, a performer. The children loved her and Saint John loved her. Without Jene Wood, why, there would be no Christmas program, no Christmas fund. Why, without Jene, there would be no Christmas.

Yet, one day, she too was gone. Off with her husband Bill Stewart to Ontario, where Bill would find national success in the broadcasting field.

And so it goes. Denny Comeau and Buddy Guilfoyle were co-hosts of the Christmas broadcast for three years, and then Dave White and Gary Murphy took over. They all brought something bright and unique to the program, but it also became apparent that the program they had built was bigger than the performers. It was a tradition—a tradition that will be carried on today.

The need, of course, continues, but it is not the same. No one is hungry.

No one—except the poor people.

And there are poor people in our community. People who depend on the Empty Stocking Fund.

I had a letter from such a person this week. She is a single mother of a seven-year-old son. She hoped the Empty Stocking Fund would remember her son at Christmas.

She had another request. She wrote: "Food would be greatly appreciated, as it is very expensive near Christmas." In our community no one is hungry—except the poor people.

−30−

A Five-Dollar Performance

– – – – – – –
– – – – –
–

HE WAS A LARGE MAN. Heavy set. In his mid-thirties, I guessed. Tall, but not impressive. He had the appearance of someone who had spent a lot of time on the streets. He hadn't shaved in days. His eyes were tired, watery.

It was obvious that he was going to ask me for money. He stopped and waited as I approached.

I, too, stopped. It was Sunday, five days before Christmas.

"Have you got two dollars for a coffee?" he asked. Not politely. Not impolitely. Not aggressively. He might just as well have been inquiring about the time or asking for a street direction.

He was a big man, but there was nothing particularly intimidating about him. He had the appearance and demeanour of a loser. But he knew this game, and I found myself thinking this was not the first time he had asked a stranger for money. I didn't resent his approach. There was, in fact, nothing to resent. He was another victim of society. There but for the grace . . . .

I stopped as he positioned himself in front of me, all but blocking my way, but doing so rather adroitly and somehow in a non-challenging way. I knew I had more than two dollars in change in my pocket. All I had to do was give him the money and be on my way. I also had some bills, and I remembered there was a five-dollar bill on the outside. Perhaps I would give him five dollars. I put my hand into my pocket.

"If I had three dollars, I could get something to eat." He had made a score. He knew it.

I rolled that phrase around in my mind. If I had three dollars I could get something to eat. I paused. I had already decided to give him some money, but I didn't want him to think I was an easy mark.

"You asked for two dollars," I said.

"I know, but I haven't eaten . . . if I had five dollars I could get something to eat."

It was the Christmas season and he was working me over. Why settle for two dollars. He had that. Maybe three. Why not go for five?

"Just a minute," I said, "You asked for two dollars, then three, and now you're up to five."

"Well, I haven't eaten . . . ." Now he was talking defensively, the slightest suggestion of a whine in his voice.

I felt the Christmas spirit slipping away, oozing out of my body, all but dripping away a drop at a time. Still, two or three dollars or even five didn't make any difference. My hand was still in my pocket, a pocket full of change and more bills than I was going to let him see.

But the game was on and I decided I might as well play it out. "If I stand here for another minute, are you going to try to work this up to ten dollars?" I asked, a bit of a smile on my lips and in my voice. I wasn't going to put him down. Fate, for all I knew, could just as easily have reversed our positions, and I did feel sorry for him.

"I just need something to eat," he said in a voice a bit hesitant. Perhaps he was less sure. Had he blown it? "It's Sunday," he said, "I've got no place to go."

Sunday. No liquor stores open today. But, no, that was not correct. The liquor stores are open on Sundays these days. There was one only a block away.

"I've been barred from the soup kitchen," he said, "I've got no place to go."

Barred from the soup kitchen? A known drunk? A troublemaker? A professional panhandler? He had said the wrong thing, and I thought about moving on.

"I haven't eaten," he said, and then his voice trailed off. He'd given it his best shot.

He'd also won the battle. The whole encounter had taken less than two minutes. I found myself smiling as I pulled out five dollars and handed it to him.

"Thanks. Thank you, mister."

I didn't detect any real gratitude in his voice, but that was all right. It was more like the monotone of a tired sales clerk at the end of a bad day.

Thanks. Thank you, mister.

Then he walked away. I wondered if he would use the money for food or liquor, but I really didn't care. In five days it would be Christmas.

−30−

FRIENDS — AND OTHERS

How Come George Dunlap Grew Old So Fast?

––––––––
–––––
–

HE'S OLD NOW. At least, he's older than when I first knew him almost half a century ago, but then so are most people.

His hair is white. Pure white. It retains something of a crinkle or a curl around the edges, giving him the appearance of a well-groomed elder statesman.

I was sitting in the comfortable living room of his townhouse on Woodside Park in East Saint John and he had gone to the kitchen to pour me a drink—a healthy, long drink of rum. Thankfully, it was in a tall glass with plenty of mix.

Back in the kitchen he poured a hefty three fingers into a tumbler for himself, knocked it back, and followed with a very small chaser of water. This was followed by a slight cough as he cleared his throat, and there was a sense of satisfaction in the way he did it.

"You don't fool around, do you?" I said, partly in awe, partly in admiration.

"No," said George Dunlap, "if you're going to drink, you might as well drink and get it over with."

An old navy man, George Dunlap obviously believed if you are going to have a tot of rum, you take a good one, snap it off, and get on with your business.

The business that evening was reminiscing.

We had bumped into each other a short time earlier, and George had invited me to stop at his home for a drink. We had known each other for almost fifty years, we had been boyhood chums, and then, as so often is the case, we had drifted apart. This was the first time I'd been in his home, the first time I'd raised a glass with him.

George was remembering those years so long ago when we had lived on Charles Street, off Garden, in the 1930s. He had lived in a huge building at the end of the street, while we occupied a house in mid-street. My strongest and fondest memories of that house were centred around an upstairs bedroom with a slanted roof where my brother Doug and I listened to Joe Louis fights being broadcast.

It also was possible to climb out a back window and slide down the slanted roof to the rear of the house where, with some nimble footwork, we would disappear into the night while my mother thought we were sound asleep. And then there was my pal, George Dunlap.

Both of us were interested in sports, and the YMCA was our hangout. George was a fine swimmer and very strong in track and field. I also competed in those sports and others, including basketball, which was my favourite at the time.

"Remember Claire Buckley?" George said. "He was a good swimmer."

"Yes, good. Pretty good, but not the best," I said, as I recalled a swimming championship I had won at the YMCA. But the next day the headline in the *Evening Times-Globe* said, "Buckley Wins Swimming Title."

I was shattered. Even then, almost fifty years ago, the newspaper couldn't get anything right.

When I asked about the error at the Y, Clark Ready, the physical instructor, laughed it off and said it was just a mistake but I shouldn't worry about it. I'd still get the first prize.

The prize was a paperback book about life saving. I was unimpressed and dejected for a week.

"Who was the big, good-looking fellow who used to work at the Y before the war?" George wanted to know. "Alan something... Alan Sullivan, I think."

"You mean Royden Sullivan," I corrected him.

"Yes, Royden Sullivan. He was a big, handsome fellow who played basketball."

Royden Sullivan. He was big and handsome. He was the boys' work secretary or some such in the 1930s, and he had a beautiful black-haired girlfriend who later became his wife. He's dead now, and if his wife is alive she's not young anymore. I'd rather remember them as they were.

They used to bowl on the old two-lane alleys of the former YMCA building, and I was one of the youngsters who would set up pins. It was a dangerous game what with wood flying all over the place, but the pay was good — five cents a string. Why, you could make a quarter in no time at all.

Twenty-five cents. That's what George and I paid each week for our membership at the Y. We'd pay twenty-five cents on account until we got up to two dollars, which, if I remember correctly, was the annual membership fee for juniors or juveniles at that time. Sometimes we'd get it all paid off before spring, sometimes we wouldn't, but the Y was understanding. Those were the Depression Years and real money was hard to come by.

By paying twenty-five cents a week, or whenever we had it, we were regular members. There were others in an underprivileged class. They didn't pay anything. It would have been better if we hadn't known, if we all had been in the same class, but that was the way they did things in those days.

George Dunlap is retired now, has been for four years. He served in the navy throughout the war and then spent some thirty-five years working in the Department of Veterans Affairs.

He worked for years with Ralph Fitzpatrick, and now he remembered him. "He was a great baseball and basketball player," George said. "You played with him, didn't you?"

It was true. I had played with Fitz and the Saint Johns in the 1940s.

"And Rip Seely. Where's Rip?" George asked, referring to the top basketball player of the 1930s and '40s.

"He's in the New York area, doing well. He comes back to Saint John every summer, he's still interested in basketball and hockey, in fact in all sports."

I'd finished my drink and George was up and pulling the glass out of my hand.

"A very small one," I said. One ounce. I really had to leave. He looked at me strangely. It was apparent that George Dunlap didn't often pour a one-ounce drink, but he poured it anyway, measuring it carefully and shaking his head in obvious disagreement.

"What," I wanted to know, "do you do in retirement?"

"I walk five miles a day to keep in shape, but other than that I take it easy. I've got a wonderful wife and she makes it all worthwhile." He spoke proudly of his son and daughter and his grandchildren.

Grandchildren! Where had the years gone? Wasn't it only yesterday or the day before that we had been living on Charles Street, when the most important thing in the world was getting our hands on twenty-five cents so that we could swim and play basketball and ping pong and billiards and race around the oval track over the gym at the Y?

Who was this old, white-haired man sitting next to me and talking about things that happened almost half a century ago?

"How old are you, George?"

George looked at me, again a little strangely. I knew how old he was. We were the same age. Did I think he had aged and I hadn't?

"I'm sixty."

Sixty! How could he be that old?

"We've still got our hair."

"What?"

"Our hair. We've still got our hair. A lot of people are bald," George said.

"Well, yes, we've got a little," I said.

"No, we've got our hair and we've got our health. It's been a good life."

"George," I said, "you're right. Absolutely right, and I'll drink to that." Which we did.

−30−

Why Are All My Friends So Old?

—————
————
—

IT KEEPS HAPPENING and frankly it's got me worried. Old men want to talk to me. They want to reminisce. They sidle up to me, grasp my hand, throw their arms around my shoulder, and then they want to talk. They are old, they have white hair, and some have no hair at all. They are wide of girth and slow of step. And they want to talk about the old days — as if I'd been there with them.

A few weeks ago it was George Dunlap, a boyhood chum who grew so old so fast that he retired several years ago. He has white hair and he weighs 170 pounds, which is about thirty over his best weight when he was a young athlete, a swimmer and a runner.

He wanted to talk about our youth together, but why, I asked at the time, had he grown so old so fast? Why was he sixty? Why, years ago when we were young, we were the same age.

A few days later I had lunch with Ralph Fitzpatrick, one of Saint John's great basketball and baseball players of another era. Ralph's retired, too, and I'll be goldarned if he isn't getting old.

On the other hand he's lost twenty-two pounds and looks a lot sharper than he has in recent years. I think he's in training. I think he may make a comeback.

More realistically, he may want to get out on the basketball floor again this fall because he's talking about another reunion of the old Saint Johns. That's the team that ruled the courts much of the time in Saint John and New Brunswick from 1939 through 1949.

There was a reunion in 1969 — the thirtieth anniversary of the first junior team that went to the Canadian finals back in 1939. Players came back to Saint John from all over Canada and the United States. They hit the court for one last time, relived some of their glory days, and then spent a couple of nights reminiscing and lying to each other as old athletes do on such occasions.

Now Fitz believes it is time for another reunion. This would be the forty-fifth, and he's going to start writing to the players who were part of it all those ten wonderful years — but I have a suspicion a lot of them will be old when they get here. That's the way it is these days. But enough of Ralph Fitzpatrick and George Dunlap. This was to have been a column about another kid who grew old when no one was looking. I saw him last week in Montreal and he isn't the long, skinny stringbean I knew forty years ago in Saint John.

Eddie Barrett. That's his name. Or Ed Barrett — Ned Barrett, really. That's what most of his friends called him here in Saint John and later in Montreal. But for some reason I called him Ed or Eddie. Still do, and he doesn't complain, so I guess it must be all right.

We started out together, Eddie and I, almost forty-five years ago in the old Canterbury Street building that housed the Saint John newspapers. We were young then, but Eddie, like so many others, is growing old.

Eddie was a long drink of water in those days. He came to work wearing a St. Vincent's High School stocking cap. Imagine, a reporter wearing a stocking cap!

Those were the days when a lot of kids wore stocking caps. Not because they wanted to, but because your mother made you put on your stocking cap or hat before you could get out of the house. As soon as you got out of the house or out of sight of the house, you'd pop the hat into your overcoat pocket or your school bag.

But not so with Eddie Barrett. He not only wore a stocking cap to school, he wore it to work when he became a cub reporter.

He didn't stay a cub reporter for long. He was too smart for that, and it wasn't too long, either, before he was wearing a felt hat from Bardsley's. He was good. A good reporter and a good writer. Soon he was deftly editing the copy of others. He had the touch, a way with words, a command of the language. He was a comer and he was going places. Which he did.

So it was not long before he went off to Montreal to join the lively, irreverent, boisterous *Montreal Herald*, that city's brash and bouncy tabloid. Something of a boy wonder, he soon was the night news editor, the man in charge. It was a fun time in Montreal journalism and a lot of talented people worked at the *Herald*.

But times were changing, and one day there was no place for the *Herald*. Its heart stopped beating and one day it was no more. It was a bright, lively newspaper, but it wasn't making money. It was drop-dead time.

Not to worry. Ned Barrett went from that job to the *Montreal Star*, where he soon became one of the senior editors. He continued working at the *Star* until a few years ago, when that deck, too, was shot out from under him. The *Montreal Star*, once one of Canada's most successful and profitable newspapers, died an inglorious death after a long labour dispute.

Now Eddie Barrett keeps his hand in, writing and editing for a number of publications. He's active, alert, keenly interested, and knowledgeable in world affairs and in the newspaper business, but last week I had a feeling that it isn't the same. How many newspaper wakes does an old-line newsman want to attend, anyway? Besides, like a lot of young fellows I used to know, Eddie Barrett is getting old. Why, he's almost sixty!

It is a strange world and sometimes I wonder, if Eddie Barrett hadn't gone to Montreal, would I have become city editor, managing editor, and finally publisher—or would he have been given the nod for one of those jobs those many years ago?

I used to joke about encouraging him to go to Montreal—which I did—but somehow it doesn't seem so funny these days.

But we must remember the good times. The good times, so often in those days some thirty-five years ago, were at the Barrett Home, where Eddie and Marita (McNulty), Elizabeth, Dianne, and Caroline would punish the piano and make beautiful music for themselves and for all the neighbours, who never seemed to mind.

Eddie tells me the family got together this Christmas for the first real reunion in a long time, and I would like to have been there, but the next best thing was sitting down for lunch with Eddie and his wife Honor last week in Montreal. It was a long lunch and a lovely one, but I couldn't help but think that Eddie Barrett was looking older than he did thirty-five or forty years ago, and I hoped it wasn't something that was catching.

I also found myself thinking once again that it was only yesterday, or at the most the day before, when everyone was young, except the old people.

Now, suddenly, irreversibly, in a mere whisper of time, everyone is old—except, damn them, the young people.

−30−

His Name Was Leslie McHugh
—"Please Don't Forget It"

– – – – – – –
– – – – –
–

WE BURIED THE DUMMY one day recently and we're going to miss him.

The Dummy?

Yes, that's what he was called. The Dummy. His real name was Leslie McHugh, but he was called The Dummy because he was a deaf mute.

Leslie McHugh was born into another era, a time of different social values. It was a time, sadly, when it was not uncommon to refer to a deaf mute as a dummy.

In fact, when I first joined the newspaper a long, long time ago, Leslie was always referred to as The Dummy. Not by me. But certainly by far too many people.

In recent years, if we had been asked, we would have said Leslie McHugh was on the maintenance staff. He was, in fact, a janitor — and he was a good one. He was professional.

And he was no dummy.

And no one called him The Dummy in recent years, certainly not in my presence. That all stopped about twenty years ago.

I remember the day. A department manager told me he was going to have

The Dummy do a certain chore and he wanted to know if it met with my approval.

He waited for my answer. My response was a cold stare.

The department manager knew something was wrong, but he didn't know what it was.

He repeated that he would have The Dummy do the job. Was that all right with me?

I continued to look at him.

"Who is going to do the work?" I asked.

"The Dummy." He said it quickly. Openly, honestly, without ill will, without prejudice. Without thinking.

"Do you mean Leslie?"

He looked at me in wonder. He didn't know the name of the man who, like the department manager himself, had worked for the newspaper for more than twenty years.

"The man's name," I said, "is Leslie. Leslie McHugh. Please don't forget it."

He didn't, and I guess the word must have spread through the building, because more and more people started calling Leslie McHugh by his proper name. It's funny. Leslie couldn't hear, but he understood!

And I think he carried his head a little higher after that. He had reason to. He was a fine worker, conscientious, reliable, meticulous.

We often said we didn't know how we'd manage when he was gone. Now he is gone. He went rather quickly at the end, and we are going to have to get along without him. It will not be easy, and I, for one, will miss his friendly greetings and the hand-and-eyes conversations we used to have, because despite his handicap Leslie McHugh was very adept at communicating.

More than forty years ago The Dummy came to work at the newspaper. A couple of weeks ago we buried Leslie McHugh, a gentle man who went through life locked in a world of his own. Along the way he won the respect of his fellow workers, and far from being a dummy, he was an intelligent professional who did his job much better than many of us do ours.

—30—

There Was Twenty Feet
and Almost Fifty Years between Us

— — — — — — —
— — — — —
—

IT WAS ALMOST forty-five years ago that I waved a reluctant goodbye to a young girl in the parking lot at the Algonquin Golf Club in St. Andrews. It was a small, unpaved lot in those days, tucked in between the clubhouse, the caddie shop, and the practice fairway.

She had walked that far, with me, from the centre of the town where she lived. I would hitchhike back to Saint John.

She wore a light summer dress, bobby socks, and low shoes. That was the attire of the time. We were in our teens. You could buy a Coke for five cents, play a record on the jukebox for the same price, the highway to St. Andrews was unpaved, and it took a good two hours for a car to make the drive — unless Father Holland, the golfing priest, was the driver. But that's another story.

A summer friendship was ending. I was a young sports writer. Soon she would begin training as a nurse at St. Stephen. It had been more of a friendship than a romance. But it had been a warm friendship of two young people starting down the road of life.

I would see her again, only occasionally, only briefly and in passing for a few years — and then life and fate would take us in different directions.

Now, almost half a century later, she was walking towards me again. It is the same parking lot at the same golf course. Virtually nothing had changed.

There is a new clubhouse, but the exterior design is much the same as the old one. The caddie shop is the same, and the practice fairway is there, just as it was those many years ago. We were about to meet within a few yards of where we had said goodbye so many years ago. The years had been kind to her. She had changed less than I. Her face had some of those unforgiving lines of time, but they were not harsh, not severe, not deep. There was something comfortable and serene etched there by the passage of time.

She continued to walk in my direction. There was a quizzical expression on her face, mostly in her eyes, and a smile tugged at the corners of her mouth but didn't quite break through. Not yet. Not at first.

There were still twenty feet and almost fifty years between us, but I knew her immediately. Partly it was her face, partly her expression. And her walk. How do you recognize a walk? How do you describe a walk? It was a straight walk. Unhesitating. Plain. Sort of an honest walk, I thought. It was the girl of my youth. All I had to do was close my eyes and the years would speed away. We would be teenagers again. The sun was shining as it had on the day so many years ago.

"Are you Ralph Costello?"

It was a question but not a question. She knew the answer, just as I knew who she was. Why didn't she just close her eyes for a moment and wish away the years? It was only yesterday or maybe last week or last month that we had stood in that same parking lot. Still, she had to say something. I suppose she had to be sure.

"Yes," I answered "Yes, of course, I'm Ralph Costello."

"You don't know me?"

But I did. I knew her. She knew I knew her. It was just one of those awkward moments.

"Of course. I know you. You're one of the McGee girls."

One of the McGee girls. How foolish. How stupid. Why had I said "one of the McGee girls," as if I wasn't sure. As if I didn't know which one she was.

"I'm Edna."

Forty years. No, more than that. Closer to forty-five. Almost half a century ago. A lifetime ago. Now it was time to be awkward again. This is where we had parted. Did she remember? Probably not. Who was that man sitting in the car that was waiting for her? Her husband? A friend? Was he watching us through the rearview mirror? It didn't matter. We were shaking hands rather than embracing. That seemed appropriate. Proper. Both of us had been somewhat reserved, I thought, when we were young. At times bashful. Bashful? Well, reserved anyway.

Now we were talking. Yes, she was living in St. Andrews again. She'd been back for a number of years. She had lost her first husband when he was forty-nine. He died of a heart attack. Suddenly. I was sorry. Now she was married again. "I'm on my second husband," she said with the kind of nervous or uncertain laugh that you would expect with that kind of a remark.

That was the man in the car. With the motor running. I thought it best to say hello to him. Gordon Higgins. A big man. Big smile. It was a hot day and he thought we should have a beer.

Gordon was all right.

Soon we were sitting on their sundeck overlooking the magnificent view of what I think of as the inner harbour at St. Andrews.

Yes, there were children, and now she's a grandmother. Soon there would be another grandchild. No longer was she the teenager, nor was I. The clock would not turn back except in memory and then but briefly. Reality was all around us.

Gordon brought me a second beer, and as a hornet buzzed around my glass he told me to be careful. He is a retired doctor and he recalled the incident of a man who had drunk a beer with a hornet in it. The hornet, in a final defiant act of retaliation, stung the man in his throat while being washed down with the beer. It was one of those freak cases. The throat blew up like a balloon and the poor man suffocated.

"Will you have another beer, Ralph?"

"No," I replied. "No, thank you. I've had two. That's plenty."

Yep, Elbows Mooney
Has Still Got the Moves

THERE HE WAS, Old Elbows Mooney, moving deftly in and out of the crush. In my imagination he reminded me of a basketball player working the keyhole, pivoting first to the right and then moving swiftly over to the left and now back to the centre. Were his elbows up in something of a protective position, or was that, too, just my imagination playing tricks?

No, it wasn't my imagination. Those were the moves of an old basketball player. He had slipped into the slot and I could all but see him under the basket in the gymnasium at the CYO [Catholic Youth Organization] Centre on Cliff Street.

Ignoring the cries from the crowd, concentrating on the job that had to be done, Elbows Mooney moved back and forth across what I now saw as a zone defence of opposing players. Someone sprawled under his feet, but he sidestepped neatly, kept his balance and his position, never missing a beat.

Were we in fact back in that old gym where we had played midget, juvenile, and junior basketball against each other more than forty years ago?

No, not quite.

Mind you, Elbows Mooney was performing—but it was hardly basketball. Elbows is older now but I thought he moved pretty well for a big man. He's bigger. Larger. Those Catholic priests have a way of losing their boyish figures if they aren't careful. Yes, that's his game now. He's Rev. John F. Mooney of the Church of Our Lady of Perpetual Help at Rothesay, and on this particular day he was performing three christenings, so the front of the church was rather crowded.

Those cries from the crowd weren't from fans ringed around the running track at the CYO gym, but the whimpers and wails of infants and the young sisters and brothers of the infants. And when someone sprawled under his feet it wasn't an opposing basketball player but a three-year-old child who strolled about the church through much of the ceremony.

I hadn't seen Father Mooney in years. I wondered if he knew those of us from the YMCA and later the Saint Johns used to call him Elbows Mooney? I wondered if his parishioners knew?

I wondered if he remembered the punishment he used to dish out under the basket and in the corners in those days of our youth? And if he remembered, how many Hail Marys had he said in penance? Those elbows used to hurt a lot, you know.

Those were the basketball glory days at the CYO, back in the 1930s and into the 1940s. Originally it had been the YMCI [Young Men's Catholic Institute], and the teams of the 1930s had players like big Ray Lawlor, Nick Kennedy, the Conlon brothers, Charlie Whelly, Jack and Dan Kirk, and a good number I should remember but don't.

And then came the great junior teams. Father Mooney played with Ted Owens, Bill Ritchie, Paul Byrne, Bill Lawlor, Ralph Lawless, Esmonde Barry, Harold Horgan, Ken Davis, Ken Everett, Stu Lee, and how many am I forgetting?

Ted Owens went on to UNB, where he teamed on guard in the early 1940s with Ed Mitton as one of the finest defensive pairs this province has ever seen. They're both in the New Brunswick Sports Hall of Fame as members of that great UNB Varsity team of almost forty years ago.

Others who played on the UNB team that capped its outstanding record by winning the Canadian intermediate championship in 1945 were Keith Sidwell, Gerry Lockhart, Neil Elgee, Art Demers, and Dave Stothart. Howie Ryan was the playing coach.

Bill Ritchie had the same kind of success when he went to St. Francis Xavier University, where he was captain of a team that was largely made up of imports from the United States.

Cliff Warner, it seems to me, was the manager of a number of those CYO teams, and there was no love lost when the YMCA or the Saint Johns moved into the Cliff Street gym.

Most every game was considered a grudge match, and up there, hanging over the railing at either the CYO or the YMCA, you'd be sure to find George Hetherington, the wildest, loudest, most enthusiastic basketball fan this city has ever seen. He loved the action. He loved to see the elbows fly in the corners. He came to see the fights and he was in ecstasy when blood was spilled, as it was occasionally.

But, oh, that was so long ago. Another time. Another era. Another trip down memory lane.

Still, I couldn't help thinking that Father Mooney had some good moves for a big man as he slipped back and forth across the line of parents, godparents, and infants, not to mention an occasional stray child underfoot, blessing the children and quietly reminding the parents and godparents of their responsibility in the Christian upbringing of the young children.

I smiled as I found myself thinking that no one had better get in his way. He still carried the elbows a little high.

Later, after the ceremony, I had an opportunity to talk briefly to this big man whose smile radiates a warmth all its own, and we thought about those days so long ago and remembered some of our old friends, and we wondered where others had gone.

And then, just before we parted, Father Mooney gave me a light jab in the stomach — come to think of it, that was the lightest jab I ever got from him — and he observed that those basketball days had been great fun "if you watched out for the elbows under the basket."

He smiled and made a fast pumping movement with both arms the way he used to do back in his days at the CYO.

Old Elbows Mooney hadn't forgotten.

—30—

Jack Rector: A Smile on His Lips, a Twinkle in His Eye

- - - - - - -
- - - - -
-

JACK RECTOR was not the kind of a man who stood out physically in a crowd — and not mentally either, he would have said, with a smile that almost always was tugging at the corners of his lips and twinkling in his eyes. But there he would have been wrong.

Jack Rector did stand out in a way all his own. He went through life caring and working for the welfare of others. Jack Rector reminded you of a slightly overgrown teddy bear, short of stature and in later years round of girth, but he did stand out among his peers.

All of his life he was involved in community work, in the service of his neighbours and his fellow man. He was a thoroughly nice man, and it was a joy to know him.

He believed in people and in the ultimate goodness of people. When he retired several years ago after forty-four years of service with the Bank of Nova Scotia and a wartime stint in the Royal Canadian Navy, he said that in all of his banking experience he had found that ninety-nine per cent of people were honest.

That, many of us would think, was an exaggeration of the heart, and maybe it was, but Jack Rector believed that goodness and honesty were there to find. All you had to do was look for them. All you had to do was give the other fellow a chance to demonstrate his honesty. For Jack Rector it worked more often than not because he had a successful career in the bank and in every community where he ever lived.

When he was a teenager in the small Nova Scotia community of River Hebert, he served as a Cub pack leader and set a course of service that he was to follow all through his business career and his life.

He believed in his fellow man. He believed in the community where he lived and he believed in such organizations as the United Way. He worked for many fundraising organizations in key capacities in Ottawa, Fredericton, and Saint John. He also respected the views of others, and even while serving as United Way campaign chairman in Saint John and preaching the United Way concept, he worked on fundraising campaigns for non-member organizations such as the Salvation Army — because, well, Jack Rector believed they had a job to do, too.

Jack Rector loved to tell stories and he told them well, usually about the little people he had met in his banking career — the little people who so often would take their problems to the friendly bank manager.

There were two stories he told at the time of his retirement as a manager of the main branch of the Bank of Nova Scotia in Saint John some fourteen years ago. If you read them carefully, you'll all but hear him talking, because this was the Jack Rector that so many people knew and appreciated.

One story involved an elderly couple from a rural area who used to withdraw every cent and carry it out of the bank. About an hour later they would return with all the money. Mr. Rector was curious so he followed them one day.

"They carried the money down the street to a doorway covered with a canopy. They stopped in the shade, counted the money carefully — every penny of it. And back they came to the bank, to trust us again until the next time," he recalled.

Then there was the time the elegant and elderly lady stomped into the manager's office, glared at him, and said, "Mr. Rector, I don't think much of your judgment."

He offered her a chair and said, "Well — I don't believe I know you, but tell me about it. What have I done?"

She proceeded to tell the story.

"My niece came to you after her husband's death for investment advice. We considered your advice so wise that my nephew moved his business account to your bank and also asked for advice. What you told him, Mr. Rector, was diametrically opposed to the advice you gave my niece!"

"This is true," he remembered. "But your niece is a young widow with small children. My advice was to invest in only the best and safest, to insure her income. Your nephew is a successful young businessman and can afford to take a chance on promising investments. In my advice to him there was much wider scope."

She stared at him a minute, and rose to leave. "I'm a stupid old woman!" she said.

Jack Rector died this week after a long and useful life. His family and friends will miss him sorely, but they also will reflect with pride and happiness on a life that was so well spent.

−30−

It Wasn't Relaxing and Murray Wasn't Murray

— — — — — — —
— — — —
—

THERE IS NO WAY to put it delicately. There is no soft language to describe the man. He was loud, offensive, self-centred, inconsiderate, and aggressive. He sat sprawled in a swivel chair in the Air Canada Lounge at the Toronto airport, his feet stretched out leisurely for his own comfort and as a hazard to all others.

He shared a small table with two other men. It was uncertain whether the three of them were together, but it was obvious that he knew at least one of the men he sat with. The lounge was crowded. Weary travellers sat with strangers, just to get a seat, to have a drink, to relax while waiting for plane time.

But it was impossible to relax.

He was a real yahoo from the West. He was cowboy or football big. He was bigmouth loud.

His voice carried to every corner of the room. It pounded ceaselessly like ocean waves. It reverberated off the walls. His voice was like something I had never experienced before. I was not alone. Others glanced in his direction and shook their heads in disbelief.

He was a big man, a big man with a round face and a round body. He was well dressed and looked successful—but sounded like a bum in a Brooklyn bar. He was talking to one of the men at his table but in reality he was talking to everyone.

"I'm the bagman," he said "the chief bagman." He named a political party and a western province but why embarrass the party by identifying it in this story? Both Brian Mulroney and John Turner have enough to worry about these days without being associated with this yahoo.

"So you got married again," he said, in what seemed to be partly a question and partly a statement.

His companion's answer, if indeed he gave an answer, was not something anyone a table away would have heard.

"How much of a hiatus was there?" the Loud One wanted to know. "Hiatus," he repeated. "How much of a hiatus? How much time between marriages?"

And then, "That's all, eh? Is that enough? I mean is that enough time between two women, between two marriages?"

No question, it seemed, was too personal, too delicate. "You've gone white," he said to the man who indeed had white hair. "You're pure white. Maybe the new wife's too much for you."

The Big Man laughed. His companion did not join in.

"What happened to the kids? Do you get to see the kids? Does she let you see the kids?"

It was like listening to one part of a telephone conversation — a telephone conversation you would rather not hear, but one you could not avoid.

Now, turning to business, he continued his cross-examination. "If you're a partner in the firm why isn't your name on the letterhead? I saw some of the stationery and your name wasn't on it. I thought your name would be on the letterhead.

"Well, if you're a partner why don't you just put it on. It's important. If you're a partner you should be listed on everything. Believe me, it's important. It makes a difference. Why don't you put it on, then?"

Incredible. Unbelievable. He was loud, offensive, ignorant. A bully, I decided.

Now he was back to the family. "How young is your new wife? How about kids? Any new kids?"

Then, suddenly, mercifully, there was silence. I glanced up and the big yahoo was heading in our direction. I was sitting at a small table with a man I didn't know. We had nodded when I sat down but neither of us felt it necessary to introduce ourselves. He was reading his newspaper. I was reading mine.

The man from the West, the big-time operator with the ring announcer's voice apparently was coming over to check the departure screen behind us. As he neared our table his eyes lit up in recognition.

"Murray," he said, extending his hand, "Murray . . . ." The man sitting across the table from me looked up from his newspaper and said, "I'm not Murray."

That was all. "I'm not Murray." He resumed reading his newspaper.

The yahoo stopped and looked at the man, who continued reading his newspaper. "Well, I'll be darned," he said. "You sure look like Murray, but I haven't seen him for years. But you look like him . . . you remind me of Murray."

The man who wasn't Murray didn't look up, but he murmured, "No, I'm not Murray."

"Holy old expletive deleted," the yahoo shouted as he glanced up at the screen showing departure times. "I've missed my plane. My plane's gone." He turned quickly and walked back to his table, calling to one of the attendants behind the bar: "Bring me another drink. I've missed my plane."

The man across the table from me glanced up from his newspaper and our eyes met. For a brief second there was a degree of silent communication that hadn't been there before.

I sensed that both of us were trying not to smile. "I've got a strange feeling that you are Murray," I ventured.

He said nothing immediately but after a few seconds he spoke: "I never could stand that SOB," he said.

He resumed reading his newspaper.

He'd made my day.

A Tia Maria for the Lady,
a Brandy for the Baby

– – – – – – –
– – – – –
–

"THEY SHOULD GIVE IT SOME BRANDY."

"I beg your pardon?"

"Some brandy. They should give it some brandy. That would put it to sleep."

She was a small woman with tired eyes and hair that was trying boldly to be blond but not quite making it. She wore a black turtleneck sweater and a heavy chain-clinking necklace. She was on the wrong side of forty. Maybe fifty, but then who isn't these days?

"Brandy?" I asked.

"Yes, the baby. They should give it some brandy. That will stop it from crying. That'll put it to sleep. They should put some brandy in its milk."

"Ummmmm...."

I really didn't care. The crying hadn't bothered me, at least not until she mentioned it. Now I had a crying baby across the aisle and a woman with a grating voice on my left.

"Did you get on at Toronto?"

"What?"

"Did you get on at Toronto? At the Toronto airport?"

"Yes."

"I came from LA."

I hate people who say LA, so I didn't bother to answer.

"It's cold up here in Canada."

It was a statement of fact, but it was obvious she was waiting for an answer. Instead, I closed my eyes.

"I mean, it's cold for people from LA. I'm from Canada myself. Originally, that is. So I don't mind the cold that much."

My eyes remained closed.

"I don't like going back to Montreal anymore, but I have to sometimes to see my relatives. The last time I was there I had to identify a rapist at a trial. He said he'd get even with me when he got out, but they gave him fourteen years, so I don't have to worry about that. Not for a long time anyway. They don't let them out early in Canada, do they?

"I say, they don't let them out of prison early, do they?"

"Yes, they do," I replied. "The parole people often let prisoners out before they serve their time."

"Well, they wouldn't let him out. The judge wouldn't let them, not after what he said about getting me and all.

"Besides, the judge knows I'm from Montreal because they had to bring me back from LA to testify at the trial. She was my girlfriend, the one that was raped, and I had to identify the guy that did it. I didn't know him personally, but I'd seen him with her . . . not when he was doing it. I wasn't there or anything. Not right at the time.

"But it wasn't so bad, the trip I mean. My mother died and I had a free trip back for the funeral. I mean, they didn't bring me back for the funeral. They brought me back for the trial and my mother died at the same time, so I was able to go to the funeral, and the judge postponed the trial because I was all broken up and couldn't testify. So I had my plane ticket paid for and I stayed at a hotel, and they paid for that, too. So I had all my expenses paid.

"Oh, I had to buy a black dress for the funeral, but that was all it cost me. I've got plenty of black dresses in LA, but I didn't bring them with me. Besides they're mostly cocktail dresses, low cut, you know, so I wouldn't wear one of them at a funeral. Not unless it was someone in show biz in LA. Do you know anyone in show biz?"

"No."

"Oh. Well, I don't know any really big stars personally, but I know some singers and dancers that I hang around with, you know.

"Anyway, they wouldn't let him out early because he was very brutal when he did it. It wasn't just a plain rape, you know."

She was back on the rape business. I opened my eyes and she apparently took this as a sign of renewed interest. She smiled a smug smile to let me know she wasn't worried.

"Are you staying in Montreal?"

"No."

"Oh."

She ordered a Tia Maria and lit up a long, thin, cigar-cigarette. I think they're called cigarettos. Something like that.

"Do you smoke?"

"No."

"Don't you drink, either?"

"No," I lied.

She was silent for the rest of the trip, having deduced that I was a pretty dull stick.

The baby had stopped crying.

"I think they must have given the baby some brandy," she said. But I didn't bother to answer.

−30−

A Dollar Store Christmas

- - - - - - -
- - - - -
-

WEDNESDAY. Two days before Christmas.

One of the coldest days of the year. Freezing, windy, bone-chilling weather.

But it didn't matter. The old man was in his car, warm and comfortable. If he wanted more heat all he had to do was push a button.

Then he saw them. A mother and two children, walking up a steep hill from the nearby shopping centre. The children, he guessed, were probably five and six. Two boys in thick jackets, scarves tied tightly around their necks, and caps pulled down over their ears.

Each carried a small bag clearly marked from the Dollar Store. It was obvious that there was one item in each bag. Their Christmas presents? Maybe. Maybe not.

In contrast, the woman — almost certainly the mother — was not dressed for the weather. She wore a light jacket and jeans. She had a sharp, pinched face, tired, all but lifeless eyes. Was this the result of the bitter weather or telltale signs of a difficult life? Probably a bit of both, the man thought, as he watched the three head up the street, hunched down against the wind. What was in those small, pathetic bags? Where were they going? What awaited them at home?

Then they were gone. The man shook his head in sadness and instead of heading home, drove around the block thinking about the two small children and what Christmas morning would be like in their home. What could he do? What should he do? At the very least, he could offer them a drive to their home. Then a word or two, spoken quietly, cautiously: "Are you ready for Christmas? Is everything all right? Is there anything you need?"

He'd give them some money. That was the thing to do, but how much? Perhaps twenty dollars for each child. Then there was the timing. What would the mother think? The way to do it, he decided, was just to pull a few bills out of his pocket as they were about to leave the car. "Here," he would say to the mother, "buy something for the boys for Christmas." But maybe it should be more. Forty dollars. What could that buy?

Now they were in sight again, just ahead of the car, walking into the wind. The woman, the mother, had to be freezing. The boys, he now noticed, had bare hands. Why did some people have so little while others had so much?

The old man pulled to the curb, pushed a lever, and the window on the passenger side of the car slid down. Once again he could see the strain on the woman's face, a face drawn and red from the wind, eyes staring at him with suspicion and distrust.

"Are you going far?"

She didn't answer. She didn't break her stride. She turned from him and looked straight ahead, but he had already read the message in her eyes, in her body language. Who did he think he was, anyway? Did he think she was born yesterday? She knew his type, and she knew how to handle them.

"It's very cold," he said. "Do you need a drive?"

"No," she said, defiance in her voice.

The old man left the window open and the car moved slowly along at their walking pace.

"No," she said. Louder this time. "No, I don't want no drive."

She marched on. Head high. Eyes straight ahead. The boys followed her, ignoring the car and the driver. Each carrying his Dollar Store bag.

The old man sat in the comfort of his car. He wished he could have given the woman something for those two boys. Perhaps there were more children at home. Earlier he had walked a single block to reach his car. He knew how cold it was. He worried about the Christmas they would have and how he might have helped.

But it was not to be.

The woman in the flimsy jacket marched on, proudly, defiantly, and probably, though he hoped not, to a bleak Christmas.

The old man watched the three into the distance, closed the window of the car, and drove away. His Christmas, too, would be something less than it might have been because he would not soon forget the proud, defiant mother and her two small boys.

And those Dollar Store bags.

−30−

NEWSROOM STORIES

Everyone Was Young — Except the Old People

SOMEONE BLINKED, and forty years disappeared.

At least that's the way it seemed that day recently when we gathered in the lunchroom to pay tribute to two long-time employees who started with the newspaper back in 1940.

Where did the years go? Why did they go so quickly? Why are all the young people suddenly old?

Who blinked those forty years away?

When Ruth and Eddie McEachern joined the company a lifetime ago, away back in 1940, the newspapers were selling for three cents at the newsstands, Churchill was a candidate to succeed Chamberlain as leader of the Conservative Party in Britain, and it was Dorothy Dix, not Ann Landers, who was dishing out daily advice to the lovelorn.

The headlines shouted "Berlin Residents Sent To Shelters Again," and "Central London Escapes Serious Bombing." The Detroit Tigers and Cincinnati Reds were in the World Series.

The world was at war when young Eddie McEachern and Ruth Evans reported for work in the old Canterbury Street building — McEachern to the composing room where his father Henry had worked for so many years, and Miss Evans to the cluttered warren that was the circulation department.

And now they are young no longer. Almost a lifetime of service is behind them. Soon they'll be thinking about retirement. Who blinked?

In those long-ago days, Henry McEachern was the company jokester. He was known as the mayor of Quispamsis long before the village of Quispamsis ever considered electing anyone to such a post. He was the cut-up at the office parties and the sparkplug for the softball team and the bowling league. He was the man with the mouth organ at office picnics and the first to jump into a Santa Claus suit at Christmas.

And then suddenly Henry McEachern was old. It was time for his retirement; a few more tunes on the mouth organ, and he was gone. But his young son, Eddie McEachern, was there to take his place to carry on a tradition — so why was Eddie McEachern standing there beside Ruth Evans, waiting to receive a forty-year watch, and why were they no longer young? Who blinked? Miss Evans is no longer a clerk in the circulation department. In fact, she has ruled over the girls in that department for most of those forty years, not with an iron hand but with quiet good humour and the matronly guidance of a kindly den mother.

But still, wasn't it only yesterday or perhaps the day before that she and Eddie McEachern first reported for work?

Her boss was circulation manager Robert Marr, long since gone and living in retirement in Victoria, as is Percy Butler, the advertising manager in the 1940s. He's over ninety now and one of the favourites, we hear, of the widows and spinster ladies who live in the same apartment building in Victoria. Maybe life does begin at eighty!

T.F. Drummie was the publisher of the day. He was known, for some reason — perhaps his flowing white hair — as the Silver Fox of Canterbury Street. Or perhaps it was a tribute to his business acumen. Don Smith, still pounding a typewriter in Sussex, was the managing editor in those days, and young Stuart Trueman, a budding writer, was the city editor.

If you were to read the newspaper in the early fall of 1940 you would have been informed that Fred Risteen had just defeated Arthur McF. Limerick three up in the 36-hole final of the Fredericton Golf Club championship. George Urquhart, later to become one of New Brunswick's most successful business entrepreneurs, was playing basketball with the RCASC team in Saint John. It was

Yank Urquhart in those days, and he was one of the province's leading baseball pitchers. As a basketball player, he was less than outstanding — but watch out for those elbows under the basket!

The Civic Improvement League had just voted to support a slate for Common Council consisting of C.R. Wasson for mayor, the retiring mayor D.L. MacLaren for council, along with L.V. Lingley, Walter H. Golding, M. Gerald Teed, Arthur E. Skaling, and a young lawyer named J. Paul Barry.

Mackenzie King was Canada's wartime prime minister, John B. McNair New Brunswick's premier. Hugh John Flemming would have to wait another twelve years before coming to power under the guidance and tender loving care of one Dalton Camp. Richard Hatfield was a nine-year-old schoolboy in Hartland and Joseph Daigle was a six-year-old on the other side of the province. Don Garey, Walter Butler, and Joe O'Toole were Saint John's famous Kid Line of hockey fame, soon to abandon their hockey uniforms for army khaki.

Jimmy Fox, destined to be one of New Brunswick's finest all-round athletes, had just completed a banner season as a midget baseball player.

And everyone was young, except the old people.

That was only yesterday, but it was also forty years ago.

Who blinked those forty years away? And why?

−30−

The Kid's First Newspaper Scoop

— — — — — — ·— —
— — — — —
—

HE WAS FIFTEEN and this was to be his first newspaper scoop.

Someone had stolen a lady's purse during a midweek prayer meeting at Germain Street Baptist Church, and there was a lot of commotion, consternation, and wringing of hands when the churchgoers found out what had happened.

Who, they demanded of each other, would do such a thing? In a church of all places. During a prayer meeting. The answer seemed obvious. Some sneak thief must have slipped into the building and made off with the purse during the meeting. Was nothing sacred anymore?

Everyone was upset, annoyed, and agitated. In fact, agitation was all over the place. The only person to blame, it seemed, was the woman herself. How could she have been so thoughtless as to leave her purse, money and all, hanging with her coat in the church hallway? But who was going to come right out and say a thing like that when she was the one who had suffered the loss?

Then there was the matter of the police, and the argument among those who thought the police should be called and those who wondered if that would be wise and whether it would do any good anyway. Also, if there was publicity, might that give other thieves bad ideas?

As the discussion went on it was watched intently from the fringe of the gathering by the boy, who by now had convinced himself that a story of a sneak thief hoisting a church prayer meeting was big news.

The boy wasn't at the church for the prayer meeting but to play basketball with members of the Trail Rangers, a group of youngsters lured there for basketball and probably oblivious to the real intent of the church elders, which without question was somehow to save their young souls, perhaps while they were exhausted after a hard game or practice session. Did it work? Did these youngsters find the path to righteousness and salvation forever? Well, maybe. But on a definite plus side, several became fine basketball players.

However, on this night in the 1930s neither basketball nor the young men's salvation was on the mind of the fifteen-year-old-reporter-in-waiting as the older people in the church continued to mill about, wring their hands, and lament the terrible turn of events. The purse had contained eleven or twelve dollars — a lot of money in those times, in the middle of the Depression.

The boy, who had been selling newspapers for years and whose older brother was already writing sports reports for one of the local newspapers, took in all the details and came to what for him was an obvious conclusion: this indeed was a news story. Maybe even a newspaper scoop. Why, he could all but read the headline: "Thief Takes Up Own Collection at Prayer Meeting."

So the boy slipped away and headed up the stairs to the second floor, where he knew there was a telephone. He wanted to be well out of sight of the prayer meeting crowd. He was young but he knew instinctively that they wouldn't appreciate some kid deciding to call the newspaper. A moment later, after getting the telephone number from the phone directory, he was talking to the newspaper and someone who identified himself only as "city desk."

"There's been a robbery at the church," the boy blurted out.

"How much are you talking about?"

"What?"

"How much? How much money was taken? What happened? What church?"

"Germain Street . . . Germain Street Baptist Church," the boy replied. They'd probably want the denomination, he reasoned. "We don't know how much was taken. It was a woman's purse. It could have been eleven or twelve dollars."

"Did anyone see him...the thief?" the city editor wanted to know. And then, "Have you called the police?"

"No," the boy said, and he was pleased with himself for knowing the answers. "No one saw him and I don't think they want to call the police...they think it might give other robbers some ideas...."

Ironically, it was the *Saint John Citizen* the boy had called, not the *Evening Times-Globe*, the newspaper that he had peddled as a newsboy for years. He felt a bit guilty about that, but figured this story was all but made to order for the *Citizen*, whose reporters were stirring things up in the city with stories about people and the Depression, about crime and families in need. Someone named Charlie Lynch had just written a series of articles about families being evicted from their homes because they couldn't pay the rent, and there were pictures of a family sitting on chairs on Main Street guarding their meagre belongings and not knowing where they would go and whether anyone would take them in. It was a dramatic story that reflected the heartache and hopelessness that had overtaken thousands, even millions, of families in the Depression. It was also one of those tragedy-next-door stories that everyone in Saint John could relate to, the kind of a story that had people talking about the *Citizen* and its brash young writers.

And now an excited young boy—all but a reporter himself—was whispering his story into a telephone to the city editor of the newspaper of the people.... "I thought I should call you so you could get a reporter down here," he told the editor.

The editor, maybe seriously, or possibly with a smile on his face, said okay, he'd get someone right on it. He told the kid to get any additional information that he could round up, and he'd send someone right along.

The boy hung up the phone and waited. He knew better than to go asking anyone for more details. No one would have told him anything anyway, but he decided he had to wait. Besides, he wanted to see how a real reporter would handle the story.

After about half an hour one of the adults spotted the boy in the Sunday School hallway and told him it was time to go home. They were going to lock up for the night, so now the boy had to wait outside the church.

He waited another half hour but no one came. Perhaps the editor had just been patronizing him. Perhaps a stolen purse in a church wasn't his idea of a story, or maybe he was just being nice to a kid who had called the newspaper. The kid would never know.

Not long after that the *Citizen*, that perky, lively, irreverent, people-newspaper went out of business, but it left its mark on journalism in New Brunswick and in Canada. Some of its graduates simply crossed Canterbury Street and went to work for the *Telegraph-Journal* or the *Evening Times-Globe*. Among them was Sandy Thorne, a veteran writer who had been the *Citizen*'s editor. He spent the rest of his working life writing editorials for the two newspapers the *Citizen* had hoped to replace. Charlie Lynch became a war correspondent and an internationally recognized journalist. In later years he would be one of the best-known and best-read columnists in the Ottawa press corps. John Fisher, a young man from Sackville, N.B., who wrote editorials and features for the *Citizen*, went on to become Mr. Canada, a storyteller, radio commentator, public speaker, and promoter of everything Canadian. One of his crowning achievements was as Centennial Commissioner in charge of promoting Expo and Canada's centennial year in 1967. Doug Costello was another young writer at the *Citizen* who would cross the street to become sports editor of the *Telegraph-Journal* before moving on to win new recognition and honours as an award-winning journalist, first in Maine and later in Pennsylvania. And then there was The Kid.

The Kid? Yeah, the kid who at fifteen recognized the irony of a sneak thief lifting a lady's purse while the congregation prayed for their own souls and, undoubtedly, for the salvation and redemption of thieves and sinners not unlike the one hard at work right under their very own noses. Oh, that kid? He, like his brother before him, went into the newspaper business while still in his teens. He started as a sports writer, then became a regular reporter, columnist, editor, and publisher in the long-time Canterbury Street home of the *Telegraph-Journal* and the *Evening Times-Globe*, right across the street from the building that had housed the *Citizen*.

He stayed around for a long time, and no matter what his position he always answered his own phone. He also paid attention when people called in with news tips. You never know, he reasoned, when one day there might be a young reporter out there with a tip on a real news story. Maybe even a newspaper scoop.

Tea and Crumpets in the Bad Old Days

— — — — — — —
— — — — —
—

ONE OF NEW BRUNSWICK'S best-known sports writers back in the 1930s and into the war years was A. Malcolm MacGowan of the *Telegraph-Journal*. He was short, chubby, and cheerful. He wore ill-fitted suits that invariably included a vest bearing evidence of meals eaten on the run as he struggled to complete a late story for the daily newspaper.

To the outside world he was Malcolm or Mac MacGowan. To those of us who toiled in the dark and dreary newsroom of the old newspaper building on Canterbury Street in downtown Saint John, he was Muc MacGowan. I'm not sure about the origin of the name, but I suspect it may have had something to do with his generally unkempt appearance.

Muc MacGowan was a newspaperman of the old school. He had a cant to one eye that gave him a look of a frightened animal. He worked long hours and was always in a rush, always trying to meet a fast-approaching deadline. The one thing that separated him from the rest of the newsroom staff was liquor. Muc MacGowan didn't drink. Just about everyone else did. When I first went to work at the newspaper I was intrigued by the amount of tea that was consumed by some of the old editors and reporters. It was not an uncommon practice for the city editor to have a large teapot in the centre of his desk. Throughout the night he would pour generous portions of a dark or amber liquid into a teacup that was always within his reach. He never bothered to heat the tea and it probably took me all of a week to realize what was going on.

While MacGowan was a non-drinker, he did have one vice. It was eating. While the city editor would spend the night sipping tea, Muc MacGowan would edit copy with one hand while using his other hand to fish around in a small leather satchel he brought to work each evening. It was his lunch box, and it produced all manner of food from chicken wings to sardine sandwiches, to apple pie and globs of chocolate cake.

But there was something unusual and gastronomically disturbing about watching him eat. He never stopped working and never looked to see what he was selecting from that little leather satchel. He would simply grope around until his hand found something that appealed to his sense of touch. Perhaps it was a nightly surprise from his wife. Perhaps he examined his lunch before he left home and knew what was there. In any event, when he hit pay dirt, his hand would emerge and he'd bite into whatever it was. Then he'd munch away while he worked.

I was a teenager at the time, and I presume that was the reason I was never offered a cup of tea. I don't know why I was never offered a snack from Muc MacGowan's satchel but if I had been, I know I would have refused. In fact, the culinary mysteries and delights of Muc MacGowan's food-stained satchel—along with whatever may have lived and died within its darkened reaches—was something he could take to his grave as far as I was concerned. Which, come to think of it, he probably did.

−30−

How to Win Fame and Influence People

— — — — — — —
— — — — —
—

THE LADY WAS GUSHING just a little, I thought.

She hoped I didn't think she was being too forward, just walking up like that, like a brazen hussy, and introducing herself.

"Not at all," I said. "That's what cocktail parties are all about."

She didn't normally do that sort of thing, but she had wanted to meet me for a long time. Did I think she was horrible? She hoped not, because she just loved my stories.

How, she wanted to know, did I write them? Did I write at the office or at home? Did they just come to me in the middle of the night or did I have to sit and think and think and think?

She had always admired writers. In fact, she wished that she herself could write, but it was a gift, wasn't it?

Did I write quickly and just do a story once or did I have to go back and do a column over and over until it was just right?

How long would it take to write a column? That is, on the average. She knew every column didn't take the same amount of time. After all, some were longer than others and that would take extra time, wouldn't it?

Did I write them out in longhand first or did I start right off with a

144

typewriter? She had often wondered why the sound of a typewriter didn't break a writer's concentration.

"I just know it takes an awful lot of concentration... doesn't it?"

Was she rattling on too much?

No? Good, because she wanted to tell me I was a writer who could make her cry. If someone had told her a year ago that something in a newspaper would make her cry, why she would have laughed at the very idea. But that was a year ago. Now she knew better.

Mind you, she had always known that writers could make people laugh. She laughed at my stories, sometimes until the tears ran down her face. But that wasn't the kind of crying she meant when she said my stories made her cry.

When she laughed until the tears ran down her face, those were happy tears. They were not sad tears. Not real crying tears.

"There's a difference, you know," she said.

I agreed. There was a difference.

Well, as I said in the beginning, she was gushing, just a little. But then, it is the season to be jolly. It also is the season of the cocktail party. People are more inclined to gush at cocktail parties, so I tried to take it all in stride.

But it can be difficult when you are being gushed to death, when there is no let-up and no apparent escape.

"I really cried. Real tears. That's how your writing affects me sometimes," she said.

"Do you realize what I'm saying? Real tears."

"But I don't always cry. I love your stories from Florida."

That, of course did it. "But I don't write stories from Florida," I said.

"You don't?"

"No."

"Aren't you Stuart Trueman?"

"No."

"Oh." And she walked away. Fame sure is fleeting.

—30—

Yes, It's News When a Man Bites an Alligator

— — — — — — —
— — — — —
—

THE YEAR WAS PROBABLY 1947 and the people sitting around the long table in the private dining room at the Union Club included Larry MacLaren, sometime mayor of Saint John and later lieutenant-governor of New Brunswick, newspaper publisher T.F. Drummie, managing editor Don Smith, advertising manager Percy Butler, and sports writers Doug Costello and Dave Pickard.

Also present were such sports enthusiasts as Elmer Ingraham, Dodgie Garnett, Frank C. Owens, Jack Chesley, and a few others whose names escape me.

At the back of the room was the reason for the gathering: Jack Dempsey, former world heavyweight champion. Standing next to Dempsey was boxing and wrestling promoter Jack Thomas.

And that, of course, is what the gathering was all about. Jack Dempsey was in town to referee one of Jack Thomas's sporting promotions at the old Forum on Main Street.

"I thought you'd like to have this old photo," said George Owens the other day when he dropped into the office and presented me with a memento of that long-ago gathering.

George Owens is a son of the late Frank Owens, who at that time was New Brunswick amusement tax inspector and chairman of the New Brunswick Board of Censors of Motion Pictures. Frank Owens was active in community affairs and was an avid sportsman. It was natural that he would be present at a luncheon honouring Jack Dempsey. The chances are he was also keeping an eye out for the province's amusement tax. In those days you trusted fight promoters about as far as you could throw them—and Jack Thomas weighed a good two hundred and fifty pounds!

George Owens was right. It was a photo I was pleased to receive, and it brought back some unusual memories.

Those were the days when Jack Thomas was trying to take over what had been boxing promoter Jack McAllister's territory. Thomas was a born promoter. He was big, blustering, cocky, fast-talking, the eternal optimist. He lived hard, drank harder, and was always on the verge of making a million.

He didn't put on boxing or wrestling shows. They were extravaganzas. He brought all manner of man and beast to Saint John for his wrestling cards. Often, in those days, it was difficult to tell which was the man and which was the beast. The ugly wrestlers were almost inhuman. Perhaps sub-human would be a better description.

Jack Thomas was not above having a man box a bear or wrestle an alligator. "Anything to fill the hall," he used to say.

There was in fact a time when he imported an alligator—or was it a crocodile?—to appear in wrestling matches. To emphasize how dangerous it was for a human being to enter the ring with the alligator, Thomas had the ring encircled with a wire mesh screen so that the alligator couldn't get loose and "eat everyone alive."

The fans loved it.

Thomas also made sure it was well publicized that a doctor and ambulance would be in attendance—in case the alligator took a bite out of the wrestler.

And, of course, there also had to be a veterinarian—in case Jack Thomas took a bite out of the alligator!

The other promoter of that colourful period in the sporting life of Saint John was Jack McAllister. He was primarily interested in boxing, and brought fighters to Saint John from the New England States and Montreal. His big meal ticket was welterweight champion Johnny Lifford.

When things were going well for Jack McAllister, you would usually find him around the centre of the city—in King's Square, at the head of the City

Market building or hanging around the Royal Hotel on King Street. He was usually telling the story of some famous fight, bobbing and weaving, crouching and feinting as he acted out the event round by round. Jack McAllister wasn't punchy. Far from it. But he was an actor and a storyteller, and he usually had both hands going to show how some long-forgotten fighter had performed in the ring.

One of his favourite stories was about the time when his boxer Johnny Lifford was refereeing hockey in the tough mining town of Sydney in Cape Breton. The fans were hardrock miners who came to the rink well fortified with rum as black as the coal they mined. They drank the rum early but kept their bottles handy in case the referee made a bad call against their team.

As fate would have it, Johnny Lifford made one of those questionable calls one night and a bottle came hurtling down from the stands. It missed its mark but Johnny knew the area from which it had come. He vaulted the boards and went charging into the stands, where he demanded, "Who threw that bottle?"

A huge miner leaned over from his seat and with his face — and more interestingly his chin — only inches from Johnny Lifford, said, "I threw it, sweetheart . . . what are you going to do about it?"

Johnny Lifford was a man of few words.

They carried the miner out of the rink and the game resumed. There were no more bottles thrown that night.

Ah, yes, those were heady days. Thanks for the picture, George. And for the memories.

−30−

Ralph Costello, circa 1945.

Top, While Ralph Costello was known for his long association with golf, as a young man he was an avid basketball player; *middle,* Costello with his brother Doug Costello (right); *below,* on his own at the *Telegraph-Journal,* when its offices were located on Canterbury Street in Saint John.

Top, Ralph Costello (far right) and Stuart Trueman (far left) with *Telegraph-Journal* staff members in the 1950s; *middle,* Costello, as president of the New Brunswick Broadcasting Co. Ltd., addresses the Chatham Chamber of Commerce about plans by CHSJ-TV for the introduction of a new English-language television service in northeastern New Brunswick in 1978. Also shown is Bob Stewart, president of the chamber (sitting); *below,* Costello (centre) receives an award for his basketball playing. He was a member of the Senior Saint Johns basketball team, the 1949 Maritime champions.

Ralph Costello (third from left)
with other staff members in the old
Telegraph-Journal building on Canterbury Street.

Top, Ralph Costello (right) was the guest speaker when Val Streeter, shown with his wife Hortense, was honoured in 1970 with a lifetime membership in the Riverside Country Club following his election to the New Brunswick Sports Hall of Fame; *middle,* Ralph Costello signs copies of his book on golf in New Brunswick, *The First Fifty Years.* The book marked the half-century anniversary of the New Brunswick Golf Association, which was celebrated in 1984; *below,* Saint John Mayor Eric L. Teed (left), New Brunswick Premier Louis J. Robichaud (centre), and Ralph Costello with a souvenir edition of the *Evening Times Globe* at the official opening of the new *Telegraph-Journal* and *Times Globe* office and press building in October, 1963.

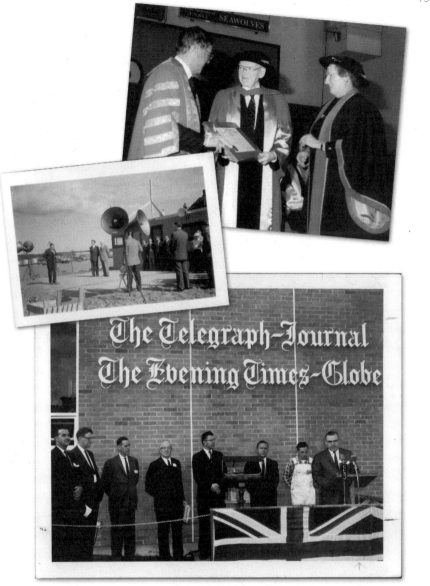

Top, Ralph Costello (centre) receives an honorary Doctor of Letters from the University of New Brunswick at the 2000 UNB Saint John convocation. He is shown with UNB Chancellor Fredrik S. Eaton (left) and UNB President Elizabeth Parr-Johnston; *middle,* Costello takes part in the groundbreaking ceremony for the new *Telegraph-Journal* building at the corner of Crown and Union Streets in Saint John in 1962; *bottom,* Costello speaks at the official opening of the building in October 1963.

One of Ralph Costello's great pleasures in life was golf, even if he was hitting
out of a sand trap. And he was quite good. At one point in his career,
he had a single-digit handicap.

A Happy Anniversary Message
to Don Smith

– – – – – – –
– – – – –
–

[*Editor's note*: More than sixty years ago Donald R. Smith started working for the *Telegraph-Journal*, first as a summer reporter and later as an editor and eventually managing editor before moving to the *Kings County Record* at Sussex. Somewhere along the line, while still managing editor of the *Telegraph-Journal* and in a moment of weakness or madness, he hired a young sports reporter by the name of Ralph Costello. When Smith asked Costello to write something for the hundredth anniversary of the *Record*, it seems he had to check with Costello several times to remind him of the deadline for the article. Some of the correspondence, we thought, might be of interest to readers who know Smith. Perhaps even to some who know Costello.

Something else unusual happened that summer. Don Smith, he of the bow tie, vest, and sometimes even grey spats, attended the sixtieth anniversary of his graduation class at Dalhousie University. How did this eighty-two-year-old Sussex scribe behave while out of the province? Well, the evidence is in the pictures. In one he snuggles up to an old classmate, Eva Mader, one-time chancellor of the University of Toronto. In another, the oldest active newspaperman in New Brunswick tries to recapture his youth at the piano. It was a grand outing, according to Smith. Of the original class of one hundred and fifty, some nineteen showed up for the reunion. Seventeen, he says, found it difficult to stay awake. He didn't identify by name the other two, but the pictures tell that story, too.]

January 6, 1987
Mr. Ralph Costello, Publisher
The Telegraph-Journal / The Evening Times-Globe.

Dear Ralph:

Re our phone chat yesterday as to the Record's 100th anniversary in September 1987, and your very pleasing consent to do an article for us and, very important also, send a picture of your good self.

As to the article — at least 500 words, please — I suppose one factor [that] will suggest itself is the key role a community (weekly) newspaper plays in the life of its community and readership area. That is merely my idea, but it seems a basic one. In any case, I will leave the subject matter of the article entirely to you.

I would like to have article and photo in my hands by Feb. 28. The date of our special edition will be Sept. 9; of interest, the first issue of the Record was on Sept. 9 (1887).

Sincerely,
Donald R. Smith

April 10, 1987
Mr. Donald R. Smith, Editor
100th Anniversary Edition The Kings County Record, Sussex,
N.B.

Dear Don:

Will you, once and for all, stop bugging me! No more letters,
Don. No more telephone calls. Just get off my back!

I know I missed your deadline for stories for your 100th
Anniversary Edition, but that's because you made the deadline
unrealistically and unnecessarily early. What's the hurry? At 82,
you should be slowing down.

Also, when you asked me to do this report by the end of March
you should have told me the edition wasn't coming out until
September. If after all these years in the business you don't know
better than that, well maybe it's time for you to try something
else.

Okay, okay, so I said I'd write something for your Anniversary
Edition, and I'll do it too, but in my own time, in my own way
and when I get around to it.

Five hundred words, wasn't it — or, more precisely, as you put
it, "at least five hundred words, please."

Don, you've got some nerve even asking me for an article. You
probably think I've forgotten how you offered me a permanent
job on the Telegraph-Journal almost 50 years ago. You said you'd
pay me $16 a week. Not only that, you sat there behind your desk
in the corner of the newsroom in that old building on Canterbury
Street and, without even blinking an eye, told me that $16 every
week was much better than the $22 I was averaging as a teenage
space writer. Did you think I swallowed that line, Don? Not on
your life. Why you even told me that if I was on the permanent
staff and applied myself I might go places in this business. Hell,
I didn't go any place. I'm still here at The Telegraph-Journal.

And now, just as if you'd never led me down the garden path, you write me one of your condescending letters saying how pleased and honoured you'd be if I would be good enough to consent to do an article for The Record and, as you put it, "very important also, send a picture of your good self."

Don, will you never change? Why not just ask me to send 500 words and a picture. Pronto. Never mind that baloney about "your good self."

If you'd done that I probably would have written that The Kings County Record has had a storied history of 100 years of service to the people of Sussex and Kings County. I might even have said that during those 100 colourful years it has served the people well and with particular dedication because it has had owners and editors and publishers who have been devoted to that task.

I confess I don't read The Kings County Record every week—though I once did when I was provincial editor of The Telegraph-Journal—but I can visualize the kind of person who should serve as editor of The Record or a thousand other successful weeklies in Canada. My idea of an editor of a small town weekly is someone who would walk through the town and be recognized by everyone—someone who would jot notes on the back of a cigarette package, or on an envelope, and then go back to the office and write two columns of copy. A weekly editor would go to the courts in the morning and cover the Town Council meeting in the evening. He'd turn out to see the high school basketball team play and he'd be disappointed if the town team didn't win. An editor of a small town weekly knows how important—how terribly important—it is to get names and initials correct. That same editor would write something very special, very personal, about someone in the community who had died and that would ease the pain for the family in a way only those of us who have done it can understand.

Finally, if I were to conjure up a vision of the editor of a weekly newspaper in a small town, I'd see someone neatly — nay, impeccably turned out — probably still wearing a bow tie, maybe even spats and yellow gloves. The editor would tip his hat and bow ever so slightly as he greeted the townspeople on his way to the office and the townspeople would think he was a little different, maybe even a little strange. And they'd be right. Because he'd be a newspaper man — and that's what makes a newspaper.

And when it was all over I'd say, There goes Don Smith. He's 82 and still writing. He's an editor at The Kings County Record. He cares about the newspaper and the people it serves — and so does The Kings County Record.

That's the sort of thing I'd write, Don — and then I'd smile to myself because you'd never know whether to believe it or not.

So happy anniversary to you, Don Smith — and to The Kings County Record.

Yours sincerely,
Ralph Costello

−30−

Collapsible Katie Had No Peer

-

WHEN MODERATOR CLAIRE LAMARCHE collapsed at a crucial point in the 1997 French-language federal election debate, bringing the television broadcast to an abrupt and inconclusive halt, it reminded Montreal's Ned Barrett of the often untimely collapses of a reporter we knew about half a century ago.

Her name was Katie Broad and she toiled for the Saint John newspapers in the 1940s when Barrett and I were starting our careers as young reporters.

Katie Broad, probably about fifty at the time, had the prim and proper appearance of a movie version of a turn-of-the-century school marm. She dressed plainly, wore no makeup, and combed her greying hair straight back. She also had a mysterious biological ailment that would cause her to collapse without notice and certainly without regard for circumstances or surroundings — even once, as Barrett recalled, before the entire Synod of the Anglican Church of New Brunswick.

Splat! Down she would go, and then, almost invariably and immediately, she would bounce back to her feet and carry on as if nothing had happened. Her swan dives were so common that her associates in the newsroom of the *Telegraph-Journal* came to accept them as normal and simply looked the other way until she was back on her feet. She was fiercely independent. When she went down — sometimes in an almost graceful slide, but occasionally with a bump or a crash—that was her business. She would take care of it. She did not want help from anyone.

All, as it were, in a day's work. Nevertheless, for some uninitiated, for a visitor to the newsroom or someone like young, part-time reporter Jack Warner, it could be a frightening experience. Warner, a law student by day and a sometime reporter at night, was not aware that, even if she fell right in your path, the proper procedure was to step over her and go about your business. That lack of knowledge got him in trouble the night she crash-landed literally at his feet. His natural instinct was to help her up or at the very least protect her modesty, as her dress had hiked itself above her knees in the fall. His intended gallantry was a serious mistake, as he was soon to learn.

But back to fainting Claire Lamarche, a prominent Quebec television personality, and her misadventure on national television, which revived memories of Katie Broad and prompted this exchange of letters—Barrett to Costello, and Costello to Barrett:

Dear Ralph:

Does the performance of Claire Lamarche remind you of anyone? How about Katie Broad staging her thrilling performance of a swan dive at the Anglican Synod?

Ned.

Dear Ned:

Fainting Claire Lamarche vs. Collapsible Katie Broad? No contest.
It is Collapsible Katie hands down. Knees buckling. Bum down. Flat out. Collapsible Katie by a prostrate country mile.
Scene 1:
Katie Broad is standing in front of my desk when I was city editor of the Telegraph-Journal. She wants to know how much space I can give her for a report on the IODE.

Phone rings.

Katie goes down for the count.

Costello answers the phone. Then, "It's for you, Miss Broad."

A hand comes up from the other side of the desk, takes the phone.

Collapsible Katie carries on a conversation while sprawled on the newsroom floor.

Conversation ends. Hand rises from in front of the desk, returns phone.

Katie, refreshed, pops up and trots off to her office.

Scene 2:

Collapsible Katie is in the lobby of the Admiral Beatty Hotel.

Legs become rubbery and she spread-eagles near the front desk.

But before anyone can come to her assistance she is back on her feet. She heads across the lobby and exits through the side door to Charlotte Street.

Front desk clerk to bellhop: "Look at that, will you! Drunk as a coot and heading right back to the liquor store." (Which, you will remember, was located a few doors down the street.)

Scene 3:

Katie does a belly flopper in the middle of the newsroom. Rolls under a table.

Every time she attempts to get up she bumps her head on the underside of the table and this knocks her back down.

Several bumps later she realizes this isn't going to work, so she crawls out, bounces to her feet, and traipses off to her office.

No one pays any attention.

Scene 4:

Katie does a swan dive in the newsroom right at the feet of reporter Jack Warner.

As she rolls over, for a brief moment out of control, her long skirt somehow hikes itself above her knees, threatening to expose the lower fringes of her unmentionables.

Gallant Jack Warner jumps forward to assist and in the process pulls her skirt back to a more modest position.

The reaction is immediate. Collapsible Katie does a jack-in-the-box recovery, springing to her feet, half-pushing and half-punching Gallant Jack out of her way. In seconds she is back in her office, slamming the door behind her.

Phones ring, typewriters jangle, Canadian Press teletypes spit out their stories, reporters report, editors edit — and Gallant Jack Warner staggers back to his desk a wiser man for it all.

Fainting Claire against Collapsible Katie? It is no contest. The mere thought of it is enough to make one fall down laughing.

Yours sincerely,
Ralph Costello

−30−

Ken Chisholm: Names Make News

‒ ‒ ‒ ‒ ‒ ‒ ‒
‒ ‒ ‒ ‒ ‒
‒

ASSUMING THAT KEN CHISHOLM has already found a typewriter in that Big Newsroom in the Sky, it would be interesting to imagine the column he would have written this week as some old pals lowered him into his final resting place in a pleasant graveyard at the back of St. John's Anglican Church in Nashwaaksis. One thing is sure: he'd have sprinkled in a lot of names.

He would have noted right off that Canon Alvin Hawkes was there, and by actual count, he would have remembered that he had mentioned Canon Hawkes six times in his column in the *Telegraph-Journal*. In fact, Canon Hawkes made that very observation himself.

Canon Hawkes is looking and feeling pretty well these days after an illness last year that had him in hospital for fifty-two days, and that's the sort of item that usually found its way into Ken's columns.

Oh, there's more that might have appeared in a Ken Chisholm column. For instance, it was Canon Hawkes who decided to enlarge the St. John's Church a few years ago and some of the members felt he ruined it — but if he hadn't enlarged the church, how would all of Ken's friends have attended the funeral? That was vindication of a sort for Canon Hawkes.

What was it Bud Bird and David Cornish were whispering about over in a corner of the cemetery? They weren't talking about the weather, that's for sure.

Ken might have put one of his operatives on the tail of that story, if he hadn't been slightly indisposed and otherwise occupied!

A newspaper man of the Old School, Ken would have smiled at the presence of broadcasters Jack Fenety of CFNB and Fred Blair of the CBC. Ken did a little broadcasting himself, but he considered it the junior service. Newspapers were his first love.

How many times had Liberal backroom operator Don Hoyt cursed Ken Chisholm and the *Telegraph-Journal* because they just didn't understand how good the Liberals were and how bad the PCs were performing? But Don was at the funeral, confiding, in answer to a question about the current Daigle-Hatfield feud, that "We haven't begun to fight."

Ken would have spotted Des Sparling, an old associate from *Daily Gleaner* days, and he would have remembered those days so long ago when a trim and athletic Des Sparling was one of New Brunswick's finest softball pitchers. Bet there are a lot of people in Fredericton who didn't know that.

From his perch on the side of a desk up in that big Newsroom in the Sky, Ken must have been smiling as he watched two publishers struggle with the weight of his casket — Tom Crowther of the *Daily Gleaner* and Ralph Costello of the *Telegraph-Journal*. Ken could tolerate publishers, but he believed that the real work was done in the newsroom by the reporters.

Say, there's Mayor Wilkins. Nice of him to turn out, but of course Ken had given him a lot of ink over the years. And lawyer George Noble. What were Noble and Costello talking about? Ken probably would have found out they'd competed against each other in swimming championships almost half a century ago, but now they were talking about New Brunswick's Nellie Purdy and her scholarships.

Charlie Woods! He was one of the pallbearers. Ken would have known that Charlie didn't really carry much of the load, but he's carried his share in his time. Charlie's old now. Must be seventy, but he looks better than ever. He started in the business in Moncton and covered the famous Bannister murder case, later joining the staff of the *Telegraph-Journal* and then on to Fredericton, where he was one of Brigadier Michael Wardell's key people in those exciting days when the brigadier was flailing away at just about everything in his role as the colourful publisher of the *Daily Gleaner*.

Hey, how about that Jerry Woods, Charlie's wife, still with a spring in her step, a smile on her face, and a quip on her tongue. Tom Crowther caught it this time. "Why don't you come over to see us, Tom," she asked? Tom replied, all too quickly, that he saw Charlie just about every week — and then caught a backhander, figuratively speaking, from Jerry, who said that was about as good an insult as she was going to experience that day! If Tom didn't want to see her, why didn't he come right out and say it? But she was smiling at Tom's discomfort. Jerry Woods hasn't changed.

If Ken had been reporting he would have noted the deepening lines on the face of Hal Wood, now the editor of the *Gleaner* and a cub reporter when they both worked on the *Telegraph-Journal* some thirty years ago. Hal wanted some information about his old pal, Doug Costello, the one-time sports writer, basketball manager, coach, and sports promoter. Costello went on to become an award-winning journalist in Maine and Pennsylvania. "Tell Doug to come and see us the next time he's in New Brunswick," said Hal.

Incidentally, Ken Chisholm was himself a basketball player those many years ago, and once wrote that Hall of Famer Rip Seely was, for his money, the best player ever to grace the courts of New Brunswick. Ken also demanded to know why Beef Malcolm wasn't in the New Brunswick Sports Hall of Fame. The next year Beef was inducted.

Was that Rainsford Henderson hobbling into the graveyard with the aid of a cane? It was, and Ken probably would have speculated on whether anyone is going to publish Henderson's book.

Ken would have approved the reception that his wife Betty gave for his old cronies at the Beaverbrook Hotel immediately after the funeral. He'd have smiled and chortled that little laugh of his as he observed that it was really his going-away party. And he'd probably have done some mental calculations on how much money the government would get their hot little hands on from the booze that was drunk. Ken liked to keep the needle in about all the money pocketed by the government from sales of the Demon Rum.

Finally, Ken would have looked with pride on how his wife, graveyard tears now wiped away, moved so graciously about the reception, greeting old friends, and remembering or listening again to some long-forgotten story about Ken and his exploits as a journalist. Now she was there at his final party, supported by their two fine and attractive daughters.

Yep, Ken would have observed it hadn't been so bad after all—for a young kid who came out of Nova Scotia with a typewriter and a determination to call the shots as he saw them, and let someone else back off when the going got tough because that's one thing Ken didn't know how to do.

Ken Chisholm believed—from the time that he wrote his first story until they lowered him into the grave—that names make news, so he might have sprinkled a final column with a lot of them. And he'd have been right. Names do make news.

−30−

Hap Osborne and the Story
of the Tattooed Man

————————
————————
——

YEARS AGO, when everyone was young except the old people, we had some unusual characters who worked at the old newspaper building on Canterbury Street and some strange people who would visit those newspaper offices.

There were the characters who regularly showed up at the newsroom to get out of the cold, to read the out-of-town newspapers, inquire about the stock market and the sports scores.

They weren't playing the market and they didn't particularly care about the sports scores. They were night people, in many cases products of the Depression. They had no place to go. Nothing to do. The newsroom, with its bare, dust-laden floors, strange green walls, and poorly lighted desks, was a haven for them. It was warm and, as a rule, friendly.

Major Christie was the editor in those days.

He was English. Old school tie. Tweeds. Handkerchief in the sleeve. White, neatly trimmed moustache. India? Of course. Proper. Not pompous. Not at all, though those who did not know him might have thought so. He lived in Rothesay.

Major Christie was, without question, a gentleman. An English gentleman.

Then there was Hap Osborne. He was Hap to everyone. He talked rough and tough. He wasn't, but that's the way he talked. He was from the North End, from St. Peter's ballpark and St. Peter's Bowling Alleys, the old Forum on Main Street. Boxing and wrestling were in his blood. He talked the language of the locker room and the boxing halls. He was, without question, a delight. He could have been a character out of Damon Runyon's imagination. But he wasn't. He was the real goods. Unvarnished. Basic. Beautiful. He was a sports writer.

And then there were the people who visited the newspaper. The real characters. Usually, the night people. They knew Hap Osborne. They read his column, waved to him on the street, said hello at the hockey games and boxing matches.

It was such a character who stood at the counter that long-ago night trying to carry on a conversation with Hap Osborne. Hap wasn't much interested. He'd finished his column and was playing solitaire.

The visitor wanted Hap to know he had just saved someone from drowning in the harbour, "but I don't want anything about it in the newspaper."

"Okay," said Hap. He hardly looked up from his desk.

"I was afraid the police might give you some information and you'd put it in the newspaper," said the man. "I don't want a lot of that stuff in the newspaper."

"Okay," Hap repeated. "Don't worry about it."

"I almost went under for the third time before I could get him out."

Hap grunted a non-answer.

"The police say I'm a hero... but I don't want anything in the newspaper."

Hap wasn't listening. The cards held his attention.

The man raised his voice. "Hap, I brought in a picture of myself... just so you'd have it."

Hap glanced up from the cards. The man was all but shouting. Hap had heard him. "If you don't want anything in the newspaper, why did you bring in a picture?"

"Because I thought you might talk me out of it, and put something in anyway."

He was one of those characters of the night.

But Hap couldn't be bothered, so that was a story that never was written. Until now. Pity.

I remember the day the tattooed man came to the newsroom so we could write a story about him. Every inch of his body was tattooed. Every inch? Yes, he insisted, every inch.

He wore a hood over his face with small slits for his eyes, nose, and mouth. He was not about to give any free shows.

He was ugly. Repulsive. But a man with every inch of his body tattooed was a challenge to any writer. Do you suggest you have seen every inch of his tattooed body, or do you just take his word for it?

He was a cockney from London, and an interview was under way in a corner of the newsroom. Hap Osborne had met the visitor, who was with a travelling circus, and was half-listening to the interview. At this point, Major Christie, the editor, walked into the newsroom.

Hap called to him: "Oh, Major, could I see you for a minute?"

The major, ever obliging, walked through the small gate that separated the newsroom from the public area, but at the sight of the hooded creature in the corner he stopped.

A look of utter horror came over his face. The major reached for his handkerchief. He was going to be ill. The circus freak's head was covered with the hood but you could just see evidence of tattoo lines around his eyes and nose. It was a frightening, grotesque sight.

The major was backing away as he asked, "What is it, Hap?"

"Oh," said Hap — innocently or mischievously, I'll never know — "I just wanted you to say hello to one of your countrymen."

The major staggered back another step, did an abrupt turn, and marched off to his office.

It was weeks before he again ventured into the newsroom.

—30—

How Could Anyone Forget
the Baron's Name?

— — — — — — —
— — — — —
—

"DIDN'T THEY CALL HIM THE BARON?"

"What?"

"The Baron. Bill Lovatt. Didn't they call him The Baron?"

A lot of people have asked me that question since I wrote recently about the untimely death of Bill Lovatt in Fredericton. Others simply have reminded me that Bill Lovatt was known for years as The Baron.

Jim Willis and Malcolm Mackay, who, incidentally, have been known as Toady Willis and Mickey Mackay for all the years that Bill Lovatt was known as The Baron, wanted to know how I could write about Bill Lovatt and not recall that he had been known as The Baron.

Len Cunningham grabbed my coat at another gathering to ask why I hadn't mentioned The Baron when I wrote about Bill Lovatt.

Why, indeed?

How could anyone write about Bill Lovatt, one-time newspaper reporter, long-time public relations officer, lifetime character, and raconteur, without recalling that he had been known as The Baron?

Jim Willis said Bill Lovatt had been The Baron back in high school days, perhaps before that. He also remembered Bill Lovatt, even then wearing the trench coat that was to become his trademark in his early years as a reporter, telling about how he crashed the Canadian Open at the Riverside Country Club back in 1939. At that time Bill Lovatt would have been only recently out of high school but already he had launched his lifetime avocation of being where the action was, rubbing shoulders with the famous, being part of the sporting and political scene.

A lot of people in New Brunswick have been remembering The Baron and incidents from his life in recent weeks. Scott Webster, who once worked, as Bill Lovatt did, as a reporter on the *Telegraph-Journal*, wrote from Fredericton to say he had been moved by the article about Bill Lovatt's cheerful, devil-may-care stroll through life.

And there was a call from Milton Bassen — that's Mickey Bassen to anyone who knew him — who recalled growing up with Bill Lovatt, going to high school at the same time, and watching The Baron develop into something of a man-about-town. Come to think of it, Mickey Bassen was something of a man-about-town himself.

Some readers may remember my reference to the night Bill Lovatt spent interviewing or otherwise entertaining or being entertained by British comedian George Formby. John Mulcahy, our provincial news editor, has good reason to remember that night. His father, Drew Mulcahy, who was the Lloyds' agent at the Port of Saint John for many years, was also a part of that memorable night aboard one of the *Empress* ships that was in port.

As John Mulcahy remembered the night, his father arrived home at the usual time, but simply dashed off without even having supper, calling back over his shoulder that he was off to spend the night with George Formby. "He just left my mother standing there with her mouth open," said John.

That must have been some night aboard the *Empress* — what with George Formby plunking out tunes on the ukulele, Drew Mulcahy plinking them out on the piano, and the two of them singing the night away, with reporter Bill Lovatt drinking in the scene and loving every minute of it. But, as he said when he finally showed up a couple of days later at the newspaper office, "It was all in the line of duty, boss."

That, of course, was the Bill Lovatt we knew. The Baron — and if he had to take his leave from this earth prematurely, there are many who would say that it was both fortunate and appropriate that he would be spared long enough to attend last summer's fiftieth anniversary reunion at Saint John High School. Not only did he attend that reunion, he mingled as only he could mingle — he saw just about everyone, talked to most of the old graduates, and then recorded the event in the November issue of the *Atlantic Advocate*.

That account was sprinkled with names and bits of news and gossip and updates on what had happened to the old grads over the years. It was probably the last public report written by Bill Lovatt, and you could feel the warmth in it as he relived an important part of his own life.

Close to fifteen hundred graduates registered for the reunion, and some four hundred and fifty attended a morning service at Trinity Church. Dr. Arthur Harrison, the principal for thirty-five years, was honoured. Tom Bell and Eric Bell and Bill Crawford were there. So were Larry Ketchum and his sister Mardi, Bill Smith and Mickey Bassen, Dorothy Ryder Dearborn and Fred Dearborn, Gladys Bell, Steve and Doris Weyman, Bill Ganderton, and many others.

That reunion touched Bill Lovatt's heart, and it would have meant a lot to him to know that so many of those old-time associates have paused in recent weeks to think about him and remember some incident from his life.

The Baron would have laughed at some of the comments, and he would have basked, as perhaps he is basking somewhere now, in the limelight of attention. And it would not have been unlike him to say, "It's nice to be remembered, but how come I had to die to get all this attention?" And then he would have laughed until his stomach shook, and after a bit his shoulders would have caught up with his stomach and started shaking, too, and soon his whole body would have been chuckling.

Then he would have looked at you knowingly, out of those mischievous, devilish, cat-that-ate-the-canary-eyes of his, and he would have repeated, "How come I had to die to get all this attention?" And he would have laughed some more. Why? Because that's the way he was. Bill Lovatt. The Baron.

—30—

The Night Dane Crosby Tippled Too Many

— — — — — —
— — — — —
—

IT WAS TEN P.M. and the city editor was worried.

His reporter, Dane Crosby, should have been back at the office an hour ago.

Reluctantly, he came to a conclusion he did not want to reach. Dane Crosby, he decided, was into the sauce. Mind you, Crosby was not a drinker. That is, he was not a problem drinker, and that, as much as anything, was what bothered the editor.

If Crosby had been known to have a problem with the bottle, the city editor would have sent out a search party earlier. Or, on the other hand, if Crosby had been an old hand at the drinking game, as so many journalists were in those days in the 1940s, the editor would not have worried too much. Sooner or later, and certainly before the deadline, he would have expected Crosby to arrive and knock out a story for the morning newspaper.

But Crosby didn't fit into either of those categories. He wasn't a lush who would disappear into a bottle, and he wasn't one of those old-time legendary newsmen with an iron stomach and a hollow leg. He was a bright and ambitious young man who looked forward to a career in journalism. Still, if he had been drinking, that could be a problem. One thing the editor did know was that there would have been plenty of liquor at the meeting Crosby was covering. It was, after all, a meeting of the St. Patrick's Society.

The editor looked around the newsroom and his eyes fell on Jack Warner, a young school teacher who, somehow, managed to teach school, article with a local law firm in his spare time, and work a couple of nights a week in the newsroom of the *Telegraph-Journal*.

This night Warner had his head buried in a law book.

"Jack," said the city editor, "shoot over to the Royal Hotel and get Crosby back here. We need his story for the morning paper." The hotel was five minutes from the newspaper and the two of them should have been back in fifteen or twenty minutes. But an hour went by and still there was no sign of Crosby and now no sign of Warner either.

Finally, as the newspaper's deadline neared, there was a telephone call from Warner: "I'm having trouble with Crosby," he told the city editor.

"Trouble? What kind of trouble?"

"He can't walk."

"He can't what?"

"He can't walk. I found him crawling up the stairs from the men's washroom in the basement."

"Did he cover the meeting?"

"I don't know. He can't talk very well either."

"Does he have any notes?"

"Just a minute and I'll check."

After a short pause Warner was back on the phone. "He's got some notes but I'm not sure that I can read them."

"Well, get back here with the notes and we'll figure out something between us."

"But what about Crosby?"

"What about Crosby?"

"What'll I do with him?"

"Put him back in the can and leave him there. We'll get him later. Perhaps in the morning."

"Okay, I'll be right back, but first I'll check around to see if I can find someone who knows what happened tonight, just in case we can't read Crosby's notes."

And that was the last word from Warner — until two hours later, after the newspaper had gone to press. There was a commotion in the hallway leading into the newsroom.

"How dry I am...how dry I am...nobody knows...."

Someone was singing. And laughing. And horsing around. Someone sounded awfully happy.

And that's what we found when we went out to the hall to investigate—two of the happiest reporters in or out of captivity. Warner and Crosby. Both looped. Both hanging onto each other. Neither in charge. Both in their cups.

"What in hell happened?" the city editor demanded.

It was Crosby who finally managed an answer.

"I think," he said, "Jack's been drinking."

−30−

The Day John Barrymore Got Second Billing

SHE WAS BLONDE, trim, and fashionable, and I found myself thinking she must have been very beautiful in her time. Now, she was moving gracefully into her middle years, still attractive and still showing flashes of the charm that must have captivated men when she was younger.

On this particular day she was charming an older man. T.F. Drummie.

He was the publisher of the Saint John newspapers, and she wanted the newspapers to buy her column.

I was the managing editor and I wasn't much interested.

So she was working the publisher. Stroking him, figuratively speaking. Pumping up his ego.

He was a good mark — he loved the ladies.

We were in his office in our old publishing building on Canterbury Street, once newspaper row in Saint John, in the days when political parties would bring out a new newspaper before every election.

Now T.F. Drummie presided over the last survivors of those political wars and newspaper wars, the *Telegraph-Journal* and the *Evening Times-Globe*.

He was a proud man. Some said vain, and they were probably correct. He had once been named one of the ten best-dressed men in Canada and had not objected when an editor told him it was a major story that deserved to be played on page one. It was, we would hope, a slow news day. However, no one should minimize his accomplishments. He led the newspapers through the Depression Years and well beyond, while numerous others challenged but, ultimately, one after another fell by the wayside. He'd operated the newspapers for Howard P. Robinson and J.D. McKenna, two of New Brunswick's prominent business leaders in the 1920s, '30s, and '40s, and in later years was publisher during the ownership of industrialist K.C. Irving.

He'd been labelled the Silver Fox of Canterbury Street and he liked that title — though it was never quite clear whether it was a reference to his long white locks, his business acumen, or perhaps the slyness that some of his detractors would have attributed to him.

On this occasion, however, he was not being very sly and not very businesslike. The lady was selling. T.F., as he was known at the newspaper and in the community, was buying. I was listening. Mr. Drummie suggested that the ultimate decision would be mine but it was clear that he wanted to please the lady who sat across the table from him. She looked much better to him than she did to me.

During a lull in the conversation, he reached into a desk drawer that was partly open and brought forth a framed photograph of himself. It was an old photo. Perhaps thirty years old. It was a profile that showed his sharply defined aquiline features to good advantage. The shading and shadows were right. He was young and, in that photo, perhaps even handsome.

"Oh, what's this?" he remarked, with what could only be described as contrived casualness. "Oh, yes," as if he had just seen it for the first time in the thirty or so years since it had been taken. "Oh, yes," he repeated. "This is the one they call the Barrymore photo."

Lionel or John, I whispered to myself, but the lady and I both knew he was talking about old-time movie star John Barrymore, The Great Profile of Hollywood's Golden Era.

"It's ... beautiful ... striking," said the enthusiastic columnist. She reached over and T.F. handed her the photo.

"Striking ... ," she repeated. "But I've got to tell you something." She paused and looked at the portrait again, drinking it all in. "I don't know if I should say this or not, but ... I must."

I sat and waited. I was watching a not very convincing drama. On one side of the table was John Barrymore, on the other perhaps an aspiring actress. I had the feeling I was about to see John Barrymore fleeced.

"Yes," she said, with a final sense of determination, "yes, I've got to tell you... this reminds me...," she paused again, and then blurted it out, "this reminds me of Jesus Christ... there, I just had to tell you."

Even T.F. was surprised. He reached over and took back the photo. He held it up to the light to see it better. John Barrymore? Yes, but Jesus Himself? This is something that had never crossed his mind.

He was speechless. Rooted there, looking at the photo of a young... uh, Jesus Christ.

Finally, he passed the photo to me. "I'd never thought of that," he said. "What do you think, Ralph?"

I looked at the photo for a moment and then passed it back. "Yes," I said, "it looks like Christ to me."

I hoped the inflection in my voice didn't give me away, didn't give away what I was really thinking... what I was really saying.

It didn't.

Mr. Drummie was too engrossed in this never-before-explored avenue. Jesus Christ! He looked like Jesus Christ. He could see it now. He was agreeing, nodding his head ever so slightly. Now he was shaking his head as if to say why hadn't someone noticed this before. She was right. He did look like Jesus — or maybe he was thinking Jesus looked like him.

He put the framed photo down on his desk. And now he spoke. "Yes," he said, "I can see the likeness... I'd never noticed it before." Then, another pause. And finally, "But it looks like John Barrymore, too."

He didn't smile. He was serious.

The lady from Toronto had convinced him. She'd made the sale.

After a few more pleasantries Mr. Drummie told the columnist I would be in touch with her shortly. I left his office and I presume she did, too, soon after.

Later she wrote to me to make what I am sure she thought were the routine arrangements for the newspapers to start using the column.

In a moment of youthful defiance I wrote back and said I had considered the column and decided against it. I don't know if she ever talked to Mr. Drummie again but if she did he didn't mention it.

Me? I thought the photo looked more like John Barrymore than Jesus Christ.

−30−

Fred Hazel: Boy Reporter

THAT'S HOW IT ALL STARTED so long ago — all but a lifetime ago
in an old red brick building on Canterbury Street in the heart of Saint John.
The building, which housed the *Telegraph-Journal* and the *Evening Times-Globe*,
is gone now, gone these many years, replaced by a fenced-in parking lot. Gone
with it are many memories, part of the history of Saint John and much of the
colour of the newspaper business of another era.

Canterbury Street was once Newspaper Row in Saint John, the street where
newspapers came and went, coughed and struggled into existence, survived
briefly, and then usually sputtered into oblivion.

That was a long, long time ago — back in the terrible, dirty thirties and
before — back when political parties were inclined to finance newspapers in an
election year and then allow them to die once the votes were in. It was a way
of life in Saint John and all over North America. This side of the newspaper
game was all before the time of Fred Hazel, but much of the background of
those storied days and the colourful characters of the so-called Fourth Estate
were still around when Little Fred arrived on the scene.

Little Fred. Some of the old-timers called him that in the early days. But if
he was small in stature we were soon to learn he was long on principle. He was
fresh out of St. Francis Xavier University, the proud possessor of a B.A. His

father was a railwayman in Fairville, a small and friendly community that later became Lancaster and still later part of Saint John.

The Hazels were an average family of modest means. They lived in difficult times, through the Depression Years, the war, and the post-war years, yet managed to send their two sons to university. One became a doctor and went off to Montreal. Fred became a newspaperman.

A newspaperman?

Yes, but Fred didn't look the part for a long time. The problem, you see, is that Fred was built close to the ground. He probably went about 125 or 130 pounds in those days. When he was twenty he looked more like a boy of sixteen. In fact, he was so young in appearance that we were concerned about sending him out on reporting assignments. There was a real danger, we thought, that he would be taken for a newspaper boy rather than a reporter.

But looks are deceiving.

Fred quickly became one of our best reporters, then one of the best reporter-writers. He was a reporter who could write, a reporter who got the facts and then made his stories sing. Fred took readers to ringside. He gave them the facts, the quotes, the feeling, the atmosphere. He didn't write about faceless people. He brought his subjects to life. He created word pictures so that the readers were there, too — at City Hall, in the Legislative Assembly, or wherever Fred was reporting.

Fred Hazel, reporter, didn't use a baseball bat to capture the reader's attention. If a city or provincial official made an ass of himself in Fred's reporting days he didn't write, "Councillor McGillicuddy made an utter ass of himself at last night's council meeting." He wrote the story. He let the story do the talking and readers come to their own conclusion. And when the story was published, readers would say, "That councillor's an utter ass." Or maybe a silly ass. The point is they got the picture. They got the message.

Eventually, Fred Hazel would take readers all over the world, to England, Ireland, Germany, Israel, Taiwan, Rome, and the Vatican. He would take readers to Broadway plays and on ocean cruises.

He also took readers with him to every section of New Brunswick — in recent years to northern New Brunswick, to the communities and homes of francophones. In bilingual New Brunswick he pleaded for tolerance and understanding by everyone. He urged the people of New Brunswick to communicate with each other, to keep talking, to try — no matter how hard they might find it — to understand each other. He may not have said it exactly this way, but he was calling for mutual respect and love. He wanted New Brunswickers to treat each other as caring human beings. And in doing this, his voice was heard — and in so many ways it was the voice of the *Telegraph-Journal*. Because of this, the newspaper had a purpose — a heart and a soul.

Fred was much more than a writer. He was a teacher, confidant, mentor, and father figure for countless young reporters. He would serve as a reporter, city editor, managing editor, and eventually editor-in-chief. Fred taught mostly by example. The first rule was to be accurate, and after that — well, you had to be read. He hated recording-machine journalism. Simply getting something on tape and then transcribing the notes was not reporting, not writing. Fred had his own system of shorthand, or maybe it was fasthand. He scribbled notes anywhere, sitting, standing, walking — in his office, at his desk, on the back of a scrap of paper, or whatever was handy. But mostly he listened and absorbed and remembered. If the facts were not in his notes, they were in his head. And if you wanted a picture of an old newsman, an old pro, all you had to do was catch Fred in his office taking a story from a field reporter — someone at the Legislature in Fredericton or perhaps a story from Ottawa — head tilted and the telephone receiver held in the crook between his shoulder and neck, and his old typewriter rattling down the tracks like Old 97. Old-time journalism. Fred kept it alive for a long time.

Fred once commented how my brother Doug and I used to make those old iron Underwoods rattle in the drab newsroom back on Canterbury Street almost a half-century ago. It was a way of life then, the school that produced Fred Hazel and Don Hoyt, reporters like Bill Smith and Bill Lovatt and Bert Burgoyne, and still later writers like Gerry Childs and Howie Trainor, who came from Moncton but still could work up some real typewriter heat when a deadline was approaching.

Fred and I were together for many years and there are far too many memories for this short piece. We went before the Davey Committee on newspaper ownership in Ottawa, where Senator Charlie McElman and others were waiting for us. I'm not sure what the senator thought about me. I guess he saw me as the enemy, although in my heart I was not. But I do know what he thought about Fred Hazel. He liked Fred. He respected him, as did everyone else. It was respect that was earned and deserved.

Fred was with me in other difficult times — minding the shop, getting the job done, presiding over the day-to-day operations during those long years when we were in the courts in the combines case against the New Brunswick newspapers, a case that took seven years before it was settled with the Supreme Court of Canada ruling, as the New Brunswick Appeal Court had done earlier, that there had been no wrongdoing by the newspapers, a judgment that acquitted them of all charges.

Fred was there again, back in the front lines, when the Kent Royal Commission came calling, determined to find something wrong, something sinister about how the Saint John newspapers and others in Canada were operated. Witch hunts? Maybe, maybe not, but they were lively, stimulating times, and it was comforting to have the support of an editor of both talent and integrity.

By nature — unless it is the 17th of Ireland or a night of celebration when Fred is inclined to think he is the reincarnation of Enrico Caruso, albeit Caruso with a deeper voice — Fred is a quiet person. There are those who would suggest he once was on the shy side — but there is nothing shy about him when he is challenged, whether it is by a Senate committee, a Royal Commission, or some drunk calling the office to threaten what will happen if his name appears in a court case. There is nothing shy about Fred on these occasions, and anyone who thinks otherwise is in for a rude awakening.

Old-timers still remember young Fred Hazel's first and only shootout with T.F. Drummie, the man who was publisher when Fred joined the newspapers. Drummie was a publisher from another era. He was a businessman and a product of the Depression Years. He had kept the newspapers going and profitable against many challenges in those difficult times and he lived by the rules of those times. He was accustomed to having his own way, and one night he made the mistake of coming down hard on Fred Hazel. It would have been all right except that it was in public. In the middle of the newsroom. It happened a long time ago and the actual issue has faded from memory, but not the outcome. Fred rose to his full height, which by the way just about matched that of the publisher, went head-to-head with his superior, and came out the winner. People were less inclined to take on Fred after that.

Fred also told me where I could go on a couple of occasions. A couple of occasions? Yes, I'd say that was it—a couple of times in the forty years we worked together, so that wasn't bad, and when we did disagree it was in private. Come to think of it, he was probably right both times. Well, once anyway.

But my memories of Fred are almost all happy ones. There were amusing times, too. There's one laugh we've shared for about thirty years. I was the publisher. He was the managing editor, and a major story was to break in the early evening. We had been hard at it all day so we decided we would take a break for a bite of supper. We went to the Riviera Restaurant on Charlotte Street, got a booth in the back lounge, and decided to have a drink before we ate. One drink. We had to get back to the office before the story came in.

Jim Morrison, one of the old pros of the news game, was on duty at the office that night, and we really shouldn't have been concerned. He was competent to handle just about anything. But this story, we had decided, needed our personal attention. This was not something we were going to leave to the judgment of the night news editor.

Then, it having been a long day, we had another drink.

Soon, as we relaxed in the quiet atmosphere of the Riviera Lounge, we began to have a new appreciation for Jim Morrison and his talents as a newsman. Soon we were wondering if we really needed to return to the office.

"Old Jim should be able to handle this story," I said.

"Yes," said Fred, "Old Jim's been in the business a long time."

Soon it was Good Old Jim and, if I remember correctly, we came to the conclusion that he was one of the best editors in New Brunswick, the Maritimes, and maybe in all of Canada. It would be pointless for us to return to the office. Why, Old Jim might be embarrassed if he thought we were coming in to hold his hand. So we didn't.

But we did have a private story that stayed with us all down through the years, and whenever the going got tough, when we were piled high with more than we could handle, I'd say, "Fred, what we need is Old Jim to give us a hand."

"Good Old Jim," he would correct me.

And if Jim is listening, up there on his farm in back of Woodstock, he should know that all of this is recalled with affection and the certain knowledge that he could indeed handle just about any story that ever came down the pike. Old Jim. Good Old Jim, that is.

There were, of course, many occasions when Fred returned to the office at night to deal with stories and with people. There was the time when Fred, the managing editor, arrived at the office to find a new reporter sitting comfortably with his feet on the desk and a can of beer in his fist. The beer was open and the reporter, recently hired by Fred, was a huge man.

Fred knocked on the glass partition of his office and beckoned him in.

Oblivious of anything untoward, the big man, beer still in hand, entered Fred's office, closed the door, and towered over the not-so-tall editor. "You wanted to see me?" he asked in what Fred could only interpret as a menacing tone.

"Yes," said Fred, and his voice could go down several octaves when he was singing or, as in this instance, dealing with a staff problem. "Yes. You see," he said, "we don't drink beer in the office."

"Oh, why not?" The reporter wasn't trying to be smart. It just didn't seem like a problem to him.

"Because," said Fred, "we had some unfortunate experiences in the past with young fellows who couldn't handle their liquor, and now drinking in the office is banned."

"Okay," said the giant reporter. He tossed the now empty can in Fred's waste basket and that was that. Another day in the life of a managing editor.

—30—

FAIRWAYS AND GREENS

When Lunch Cost Twenty-five Cents

— — — — — — —
— — — — —
—

THE PRINCE OF WALES was young and handsome, the world's most eligible bachelor. He would mark his fortieth birthday in the summer of 1934, and it would be two years before he would renounce the throne of England for the woman he loved. Ultimately he would become a tragic figure in history.

Only sixteen years had passed since Germany had been crushed in the First World War. The Second World War was still five years away. German chancellor Adolf Hitler and Italy's premier Benito Mussolini were meeting in Venice, while the *New York Post* reported that Hitler's rule of Germany was nearing an end. It was wishful thinking and, tragically, it was wrong.

F.D.R. was in his first term as president of the United States. R.B. Bennett and the Conservatives were in power in Ottawa.

The world was in the grip of the Great Depression.

And a one-time liquor huckster had just been named head of the United States Securities and Exchange Commission. His name: Joseph P. Kennedy.

Glenn Cunningham was the sensation of the United States' track-and-field season, running the mile in record-breaking time.

England's Henry Cotton, at twenty-seven years of age, was attracting international attention in the golfing world, winning the British Open with a score of 293 at Royal St. George's.

Down in Georgia, the Augusta National Golf Club had been organized and a breathtakingly beautiful course carved out of what had once been wilderness—and later one of America's finest nurseries, the creation of a Belgian baron, Prosper Jules Alphonse Berkmans. A scholar, horticulturalist, landscape architect, botanist, and artist, he left a legacy that was to become one of the most famous golf courses in the world. It was in the summer of 1934 that golf's immortal Bobby Jones, retired since his Grand Slam victory in 1930, invited some friends to Augusta for a friendly, somewhat informal golf championship. Those friends just happened to be the finest golfers in the world and, while the tournament would not adopt its name officially until four years later, that's how the Masters was born.

In Saint John, summer frocks were on sale in MRA's huge department store for a dollar each. You could take a cruise from Saint John to Boston and "enjoy two cool nights at sea" on a weekend excursion. The price? Twelve dollars.

At Wassons Soda Spa, on Sydney Street in Saint John, the luncheon special was a salad of tomato stuffed with shrimp, a roll, and tea or coffee—for twenty-five cents. If that didn't tickle your fancy, you could have salmon on toast, a roll, and tea or coffee for the same price.

And in Fredericton, the beautiful tree-lined capital city on the banks of the St. John River, the first New Brunswick Amateur Golf Championship was about to be played.

That was the beginning of organized golf in New Brunswick, but it would still be two years before I would walk up the gravel driveway of the Riverside Country Club to gaze in awe at the magnificent clubhouse, the rolling fairways, and the immaculately manicured greens—a visit that, as a fledgling thirteen-year-old caddie, would introduce me to the wonderful world of golf and change my life forever.

Thirty years later I would be president of the club and chairman of the building committee that would preside over construction of a new year-round golf and curling facility, replacing the still stately, still gracious but aging summer clubhouse—a necessary but heart-wrenching decision for the board and members of that time.

You Were Right, Harry Lewis
—Fifty Years Ago!

– – – – – – –
– – – – –
–

BACK IN THE 1930S, when I was a caddie at the Riverside Country Club and everyone was young except the old people, Harry Lewis was in love with Patty Berg.

It was an unusual love affair.

Harry Lewis, you see, was a printer at the *Telegraph-Journal* in that ancient building at the corner of Canterbury and Church Streets in downtown Saint John.

Harry was a bachelor and something of a character. He wore horn-rimmed glasses, hid behind a heavy beard, and drove a huge black boxcar of a 1928 Buick. He was a virtuoso of two keyboards. One was that great iron horse of the printing trade, a linotype machine that turned out type at the rate of three or four lines a minute long before modern technology and computers came along to revolutionize the printing trade by producing hundreds of lines in mere seconds. The other keyboard was that of a pipe organ that Harry built in his apartment. Yes, Harry was different.

He was opinionated, stubborn, sometimes obstinate—and underneath it all, a very decent fellow. He and another printer, Ed Stentiford, were of modest means but they paid their caddies a dollar a round at a time when most golfers,

many of them from affluent families in Saint John and Rothesay, paid fifty cents.
An extra ten cents was a welcome tip.

In those days of the Great Depression, Harry was in love with golf and in love
with Patty Berg, one of the game's all-time greats. Like so many other people
who are old now, Patty Berg was young in those days -- only seventeen when she
first reached the finals of the US Women's Amateur Golf Championships in 1935.
She would win four world championships, be elected to the World Golf Hall of
Fame, and become one of the greatest names in the history of the game.

But in those days, in the 1930s, she was a chubby teenager, red-haired,
freckled, and no one would have accused her of being beautiful. No one, that
is, except Harry Lewis. Harry insisted she was beautiful, and Harry was right.
Mind you, she wasn't beautiful or attractive and sexy like, say, today's glamour
girl Jan Stephenson or some of the other charmers who have come and gone on
the Ladies' Professional Golf Association tour, but she had a beauty that would
stay with her all through the years, right until this day when, at seventy, she is
one of the most respected and beloved personalities in the world of golf.

Patty Berg, that wonderful redhead of Harry Lewis's youth, was the speaker
recently when world golf leaders gathered at the Sawgrass Golf Resort not far
from Jacksonville, Florida, for the presentation of two awards that recognize
outstanding contributions to golf.

But, here, let me tell you something about Patty Berg, who is without
question a very beautiful person. There was a time, half a century ago, when
I would never have admitted that, even if I had believed it. In those days Bob
Bishop, a boyhood chum and fellow caddie, and I used to ridicule Harry Lewis's
idea of beauty — but Harry was right. He saw something that we missed.

Now it is fifty years later, at the 1988 National Golf Foundation Awards
Dinner, and Patty Berg has just been introduced to a great wave of applause
and affection.

In her playing days she was a feisty, freckled fireplug from Minneapolis
who would win eighty-four titles in her career as an amateur and professional,
including fifteen major championships. She was one of the founders and the first
president of the LPGA and for years a powerful presence on the LPGA tour. She
won countless honours, and in 1979 the LPGA created the Patty Berg Award for
diplomacy, sportsmanship, goodwill, and contributions to the game.

But now she is old. She is showing her years. She is not the healthy, robust redhead of her playing days. She looks like a little old grandmother, but she steps briskly to the podium, grabs the microphone, and in a voice and style not unlike that of Ma on *The Golden Girls* says, "I've got to tell you a couple of stories to get going."

Her first story was about the robber who broke into a home. He was a professional burglar, and he'd checked the house carefully to make sure no one was there.

He was going about his business with the aid of a small flashlight, slinking through the downstairs section of the house, when he heard a voice that said, "Jesus is watching you."

He turned off his light, held his breath, and in a few seconds he heard the message repeated: "Jesus is watching you."

The voice was in the same room. He had no alternative—he had to confront the owner of the voice. It was a strange, raspy voice, and he decided it was probably a little old lady calling on a Higher Power to help frighten him off.

He turned on his flashlight, shone it around the room until it came to rest on—a parrot in a cage.

The parrot repeated the message for the third time, only this time it said, "This is your final warning...Jesus is watching you."

The burglar just laughed. "You sure had me worried for a minute," he said. Still laughing to himself, he turned to face—a small pitbull.

And the parrot said, "Sic him, Jesus."

Patty Berg, superb golf champion of another era, told more stories that night. She also told the audience that she was spending her time giving something back to the game that had meant so much to her.

John D. Leupheimer, the retiring commissioner of the LPGA, and Thomas H. Addis, head professional of the Singing Hills Country Club in El Cajon, California, received the awards later in the program, but Patty Berg, wonderful, beautiful Patty Berg, was the hit of the evening. The sweetheart of the night's program.

And now, half a century later, I thought I should write this piece to publicly acknowledge that Harry Lewis was right those many years ago when he saw the beauty of Patty Berg, an inner and lasting beauty that was hidden to most of us under that crimson hair and those wonderful, beautiful freckles.

When Golf Was a Wiggle and a Waggle
—and a Whoosh!

———————
—————
—

MY FIRST MEMORY of him goes back about forty-five years. Perhaps I knew him before that, but if so, I don't remember it. What is etched in my mind is the sight of him standing near the first tee at the Riverside Country Club. He was off to the left of the tee and about to hit his first golf ball.

He was a young man in his late teens. A tennis player, if I remember correctly. Not a champion, but an accomplished player. He was in good physical shape, with the co-ordination and confidence of an athlete, so hitting a golf ball looked ridiculously simple. After all, the ball was stationary. A sitting duck.

He was wearing a dark blue jacket and grey flannel pants, a white shirt, and tie. The coat may have been from his high school graduation suit. I don't think it was a blue blazer in the classical sense of a blazer.

This was back in the 1930s, and young men in their teens didn't often own blazers or sports jackets in those Depression Years.

I recall the jacket because he didn't bother to take it off. Why, I don't know. Perhaps his shirt, like mine, had holes in the sleeves. Perhaps he had seen pictures of some of the old-time Scottish golfing greats who played golf in jackets, shirts, ties, and plus fours.

In any event, the jacket was reasonably loose and he was able to perform a couple of roundhouse practice swings. Maybe it was a hand-me-down jacket from his older brother.

Pete. I think his brother's name was Pete. Pete Bishop. Or was it Jack? Yes, Jack, that sounds more like it. Jack Bishop, an artist who later left Saint John to work in New York.

But this is another story. The story I am about to recall is about a long-ago day in the late 1930s when Bob Bishop hit his first golf ball. Bob, like myself, was a townie. Somehow we had infiltrated the caddy corps at Riverside and somehow we had been accepted by the Riverside and Rothesay regulars.

There were other townies — Cronk O'Brien, Bobo Carr, Don Brown, and numerous others whose names and faces have faded from memory with the passing of years. Bob and I seemed to fall somewhere in between the townies and the Rothesay regulars, and after surviving the initiation ceremonies of the day, we ultimately were more or less accepted as regulars.

Of course, the kings of the course were the Riverside and Rothesay caddies. The Steele brothers, John, George, and Tom. The Church brothers, of whom Hugh was the most prominent around the course. Then there were the Mahoney brothers, Eric and Graham and the big one we called Moose. They were sons of Benson Mahoney, who had a drug store in Saint John and later at East Riverside. There were the Renshaw brothers and the Roberts boys, Ernie and Stuart.

Jack Gilliland. The fun-loving, irrepressible Jack Gilliland. He was the greenskeeper's son and an outstanding golfer. Why did he have to die so young?

And Jiggs Miller. Yes, the same Jiggs Miller who later became the flamboyant mayor of Fairvale. He was a character in those caddy days, and nothing much has changed over the years. He led the first caddy strike and he might have succeeded, too, if the caddies hadn't got tired of it all and decided to go swimming.

But, wait. I'm getting ahead of my story, or perhaps just off the track. I was going to tell you about Bob Bishop and the day he hit his first golf ball.

Bob wiggled the club and looked at the horizon. He waggled it and looked again at the horizon. The horizon was still there. He wiggled, waggled, wound up, and let go — whoosh.

A six-inch miss.

The caddies laughed. Bob Bishop blinked and laughed. This was ridiculous.

How had he missed the ball? He looked at the face of the club, presumably to make sure it was still there.

Bob Bishop repeated the ritual. Wiggle, waggle — whoosh!

The caddies roared in appreciation.

Bob Bishop unbuttoned his jacket. That obviously was the problem. He performed again — and again and again.

And finally, on the tenth attempt, he kept his head down and the ball took off like a rocket up the first fairway. Even in those days when he was first learning the game, Bob Bishop gave the ball a big ride.

Bob and I became good friends after that. We caddied a lot together, played together, hitchhiked back and forth to town, and we had something else in common. We were befriended by two of the most unusual golfers ever to play at the Riverside Country Club. They were Harry Lewis and Ed Stentiford, a couple of newspaper printers who worked at night and played golf during the day.

Although both were of modest means, they were among the very few members of the club who paid their caddies a dollar a round. The other Riverside member who could be counted on for a dollar was Percy Thomson, the millionaire shipping magnate who spent so much money building the Riverside course in those hungry thirties.

Harry Lewis was a character and Ed Stentiford more of a straightman. Harry owned a 1928 Buick, and when Percy Thomson, the millionaire, sent a team of juniors in his chauffeur-driven Cadillac to Perth to play a junior team in that town, Harry took a second team to play as well.

Harry's car was ten years old, but it was the fun car — even if it did have half a dozen flat tires on the trip. Harry also took caddies to St. Andrews to play golf, and once made the mistake of lending his car to Ernie Roberts. Ernie drove into town and everything went fine until smoke started pouring out of the rear of the car. Ernie hadn't learned about handbrakes.

Harry had a beard long before beards were fashionable. He built a church organ in his apartment and would play it during the long winter days while he waited for the next golfing season. If he had trouble with the neighbours, it wasn't anything compared to the problem he faced when he decided to move and had to dismantle the organ, but that, too, is another story.

Bob Bishop was among those who became fine young golfers at Riverside in the late 1930s. He caddied in the Canadian Open in 1939 and not too long after that went off to war. He never did return to golf in a serious way because when he came home from Europe he had to complete his education, and soon after that it was marriage, a family, and his career.

Bob and I have met occasionally over the years, once in the corridors of the General Hospital in Saint John where our first sons were born more than 30 years ago. Sometimes, years ago, we would meet when Bob was a spectator at a golf championship, and occasionally in planes or at airports, but he lived away from Saint John and it was natural that we just drifted apart as friends sometimes do.

Sometimes when we met we would talk about having a golf game but it was never any more definite than that. Sometimes when I would see Gene Mealy, the golf champion and a mutual friend, I would say we would have to get Bob out for a game, but nothing came of that either.

And now, while I recall these boyhood memories with fondness and as if it all but happened yesterday, I find myself reading about Bob Bishop's retirement. He has served for years as a deputy minister with the provincial government, most recently in the department of municipal affairs. The story said he was sixty-two, but how could that be true? It is only yesterday, or perhaps the day before, that we were caddying at Riverside and Bob was standing there in his dark blue jacket, shaking his head, and muttering to himself as a golf ball looked back at him in defiance.

Only yesterday—and a lifetime ago

Ah, well, maybe we'll get around to having that game this summer. Or maybe when I retire. Or maybe....

—30—

Bill Hamilton and Twenty-four Bottles
of Doorly's Rum

– – – – – – –
– – – – –
–

BILL HAMILTON first came to New Brunswick back in 1949 when the Canadian Amateur Golf Championship was being played at the Riverside Country Club. He was tall, darkly handsome, had a pleasant manner, a good golf swing, and in just about every way possessed the bearing and temperament of a successful golf executive, which, incidentally, is exactly what he was.

At the time he was manager of the Royal Canadian Golf Association. He was later to be a golf professional, executive director of the Canadian Professional Golfers' Association, RCGA Tournament co-ordinator, and general manager of the Canadian Golf Foundation.

Bill Hamilton made a lot of friends in this part of Canada, and from time to time would return to renew and build on those friendships. Only last year he was back in New Brunswick for the Senior Golf Championship of Canada at the Algonquin Golf Club at St. Andrews. Together we ran that championship as we had run the Canadian Amateur at Riverside in 1975.

Bill made new friends for himself and for the RCGA in St. Andrews, working closely with an old colleague from his CPGA days, pro Clayton Van Tassel, as well as David Caughey, Bob Abercrombie, John O'Neill, and numerous other club volunteers.

Bill was one of those young-at-heart spirits who wore his years extremely well, so it came as no surprise that he was ready for a new career when he retired earlier this year from the RCGA. He was toying with the idea of writing a golf column and carrying on with international golf tours, which he conducted and which were enjoyed in recent years by golfers such as Randy Shedd, Ralph Strebb, Tom Hammett, and others from New Brunswick.

A heart attack ended those plans and Bill Hamilton's life a couple of weeks ago at his home in Toronto, shocking and saddening golfers all across Canada.

A warm individual with an engaging smile and contagious laugh, Bill Hamilton also was something of a storyteller. One of his favourite stories had an unusual New Brunswick twist. It involved Doorly's Rum, but to understand it you have to go back a number of years.

In fact, you have to go back to the days when each year the Riverside Country Club would send off a contingent of golfers at tournament time and in that group there would be players such as John Steele, Joe Streeter, Bill Davidson, Tom Drummie, and of course others of greater and lesser talent.

Athletes all, these golfers took their tournaments seriously. While others might be inclined to relax and perhaps even carouse after a hard day on the links, the Riverside group avoided the grape like the plague — except for medicinal reasons, of which, come to think of it, there were many.

Firm believers in the ounce-of-prevention school, the Riverside group would partake of certain spirits in the evening in their motel rooms to guard against malaria if they happened to be playing in the mosquito jungles of the Moncton Golf Club, or perhaps snake bite in other sections of the province.

They were generous to a fault in sharing their magic potions within their own group and with other golfers who might be seized with a craving for some protective medicine at almost any hour of the night. That is, most of them were generous. Joe Streeter was in another category. He might have been generous, but that is something we will never know. Joe, you see, came each year to the championship with something known as Doorly's Rum. Joe swore by it. The greatest thing since penicillin. Joe's friends swore, too — at Joe.

Doorly's just wasn't their cup of tea. It wasn't their drink of rum, either. They ignored Joe's bottle. They poured it down the sink if Joe insulted them by filling their glasses. If it was Doorly's or malaria — they'd take the malaria.

Which, I guess, sets the scene for Bill Hamilton.

Now we go back to 1975, when Bill was in Saint John for the Canadian Amateur Golf Championship. The day was over and we were relaxing at the motel, and Bill Hamilton was telling us about the most unusual cocktail party he had ever attended.

It was a good number of years ago and Bill was touring Canada on behalf of the old "I-Beat-The-Champ" golf promotion.

There was a generous sponsor so Bill was staging a cocktail party in each province. In Nova Scotia he had asked an old golfing acquaintance to arrange such a party.

Bill arrived at the hotel in Halifax just before the reception was to begin and found himself face to face with two dozen bottles of rum. "It was something called Dooly's Rum, I think," he recalled. "Doorly's," he was corrected.

"Yes, that was it — Doorly's Rum."

But that's all there was. Doorly's Rum. There wasn't any scotch, no gin, no rye...just Doorly's Rum.

Bill Hamilton couldn't believe his eyes. He was beside himself.

"Where," he demanded, "where is the rest of the liquor? Where is the gin and scotch?"

His friend just smiled and replied, "Oh, we all drink rum down here in Nova Scotia."

"And, you know," Bill recalled, "he was right. They all drank rum in Nova Scotia. At least they did that night."

"But personally," he added, "I don't know how they did it. I thought that Doorly's Rum was terrible."

Which brings us to the New Brunswick twist in the Doorly's Rum story.

Joe Streeter, you see, was the Riverside chairman of the 1975 Canadian Amateur, and one night Bill Hamilton, without any knowledge of Joe's involvement with Doorly's Rum, was telling his story to put in time while waiting for Joe and Judy Streeter to arrive and join us for dinner.

So we set it up for Bill to tell his story all over again once Joe arrived, with emphasis on how terrible the rum really was.

Bill Hamilton repeated his story, the punch line this time being, "It was something called Doorly's Rum. And it was terrible."

At which we all pounded our knees, fell off our chairs, and rolled on the floor. That is, all of us except Joe, but then he doesn't have much of a sense of humour anyway.

They held an old-fashioned Irish wake for Bill Hamilton last week, the kind he would have enjoyed. I sure hope someone broke out a bottle of Doorly's Rum, for old times' sake.

−30−

Walking the Augusta Fairways
with Sarazen and Nelson

— — — — — — —
— — — — —
—

HE WAS A LITTLE GNOME of a person, somewhat dishevelled, and he looked like someone who had not had time to change or freshen up after a long plane trip.

He was old but he moved quickly, all but trotting across the ballroom of the Ontario Room at the Royal York Hotel in Toronto.

He was nimble of foot, gliding around the dinner tables as he made his way to the dais, where he told the president of the Royal Canadian Golf Association that he was there to crash the party.

"Where do I sit?" he asked.

Robert Trent Jones, one of the world's greatest golf course architects, had arrived.

His few remaining wisps of hair were in disarray, his eyes were watery, the way eyes become when you are very old—but there's still a lot of sparkle in them, and a lot of mischief.

There was also fun and mischief in his voice—a voice that soon would take us back to the early days of his career.

Robert Trent Jones wasn't really crashing the party, which happened to be the 1980 Annual Dinner of the RCGA. He was a specially invited guest, and he had good reason to be there.

The RCGA was giving posthumous recognition that night to another great figure in golf architecture—Stanley Thompson, who, by the time he died in 1952 at the age of fifty-eight, had designed over two hundred golf courses in Canada, the United States, Brazil, Colombia, and the British West Indies.

Jones and Thompson had been friends, partners, and pioneers in golf course architecture. When they first met, Thompson had already been in the business for a quarter of a century and possessed an international reputation.

They worked together during the difficult Depression Years. No one had any money—including Jones and Thompson.

Jones, in an address to the RCGA Dinner, recalled that he had been the serious member of the partnership, the one who did the worrying.

Thompson was more flamboyant, with a devil-may-care outlook on life. Like Walter Hagan, he believed that you only go this way once and you should stop to smell the flowers.

He was also a firm believer that you didn't have to be a millionaire to live like one.

Jones recalled, "We were broke. The bankers were chasing us and we didn't have any work—but even though we were broke, Stanley would give the doorman at the hotel his last five dollars."

"'He really needs that money,' he'd tell me.

"We needed it, too, but that didn't seem to occur to Stanley. With him, it was easy come, easy go."

Jones recalled that, for a period in their partnership, he was living in New York and Thompson in Canada. They developed what they considered a rather sophisticated system of banking, which required a very close watch on when cheques were received and cashed. Nothing dishonest, but sometimes the real money was a little late in catching up with the cheques.

"Finally, the bank manager called me and suggested that we take our business elsewhere. He had been looking into our finances and he told me he was quite sure his bank could survive without our business. With it? Well, that was another matter, and not something he wished to discuss.

"I called Stanley in Canada to give him the bad news, and he told me there was no problem. All I had to do was to find a new banker.

"'But we haven't got any money to open an account,' I told him. 'Don't worry,' he said, 'I'll send you a cheque.'"

On that evening in Toronto in the winter of 1980 I realized that Robert Trent Jones was not only the world's leading golf course architect, but also one of golf's great historians and storytellers.

Now this unusually gifted man has put together a collection, *Great Golf Stories*, about the players, the history of golf, the courses, the championships, and the humour of the game. The book has a special appeal for me because, on one hand, I have long admired the work of writers such as Red Smith, Art Buchwald, John Keiran, Grantland Rice, Ring Lardner, Henry Longhurst, Herbert Warren Wind, and others who appear in this collection; while in another capacity, I have had the opportunity and pleasure of witnessing the play of golf's greatest players, from eighty-year-old Gene Sarazen, down through the Ben Hogan and Sam Snead era, and more recently the modern giants of the game such as Arnold Palmer, Jack Nicklaus, Lee Trevino, and Tom Watson.

But this book is so well done and so beautifully written that you do not have to be a golfer, or even a follower of the game on television, to enjoy what is a behind-the-scenes tour of a fascinating sport and the glamorous people who play it.

Robert Trent Jones introduces each chapter from an armchair of personal knowledge and experience and with a lucid style of writing that will add much to the reader's knowledge of the game and enjoyment of the book.

Robert Trent Jones recalls that his namesake, the immortal Bobby Jones (no relation), called golf The Greatest Game, and in a section introducing the book he remembers the close association he enjoyed with Bobby Jones over a long period of time.

Some hint of the scope of the book is contained in titles of the individual chapters, which include: "The Grand Slam," by Herbert Warren Wind; "28 Holes in 100 Strokes," by Gene Sarazen; "The Greatest Years of My Life," by Ben Hogan; "The Maddening First Hole," by Arnold Palmer; "The Longest Year," by Jack Nicklaus; "A Braw-Brawl for Tom and Jack," by Dan Jenkins—the story of the historic head-to-head, two-man confrontation for the British Open at the Turnberry Golf Club in Ayrshire in 1977 (remember who won?).

Stories by and about golf's greats are what you would expect to find in this remarkable book. What you might not expect, but will find anyway, is a delightful story about plans for golf in Russia entitled, "Workers, Arise! Shout

Fore!" It is written with wit and charm by the urbane Alistair Cooke, who is better known to millions of television viewers for his appearances to introduce *Masterpiece Theatre.*

Any regular reader of the *New York Times,* and many who do not read it but have knowledge of it, would know that James Reston is one of the most distinguished editors, a long-time head of its Washington bureau and a vice-president of the newspaper. What may come as a surprise is that one of the chapters in *Great Golf Stories* is by Scotty Reston. It is a story — "Napper Campbell Takes the Stand" — that was written almost fifty years ago as Reston was starting his career as a reporter in Ohio, and it stands the test of time.

There are many warm moments in the book for me, because I can associate with the writers, the people, and the incidents. When Robert Trent Jones writes that golf has been his life ever since he "scuffed up a dusty entrance road to the Country Club of Rochester and, cap in hand, awaited my first caddie assignment," thousands of former caddies will remember similar experiences.

For me, it was a long walk up the hill at the Riverside Country Club, almost fifty years ago, past the imposing and forbidding Country Club building, and on to the pro shop, where caddies were subjected to a fierce and challenging assessment by assistant pro and caddie master Sid Stewart. And it was with cap in hand, literally or figuratively, depending on whether one had a cap, that we waited for Sid to hand out the assignments of the day in language that would make a longshoreman blush. This was the same Sid Stewart who, mellowed with age, became Mr. Nice Guy in later years as manager of the Riverside Club.

There are other personal memories for me in this wonderful book. In 1981, as president of the Royal Canadian Golf Association, I followed two of golf's living legends, Gene Sarazen and Byron Nelson, as they performed the traditional opening-day ceremony of leading the field on the first day of the Masters at the Augusta National Golf Club.

That in itself was a memorable thrill, and so was my walk along the fairway of the par-five fifteenth hole where, in 1935, Sarazen holed out his second shot to gain three strokes on front-running Craig Wood, enabling him to tie Wood and then win the championship in the playoff.

I have even more poignant memories of Byron Nelson, whom I watched play at Augusta for the first time in some thirty-five years. There are numerous passages in the book that bring back thoughts of Byron Nelson at the peak of his playing career in the 1940s.

Nelson and Jug McSpaden, who won the Canadian Open at the Riverside Country Club in 1939, were known as the Gold Dust Twins in the 1940s, but Nelson was the superior player. Nelson won eleven straight professional tournaments in 1945 and a total of nineteen during the season, records that will probably remain in the books for all time.

A story of Nelson's accomplishments by Al Burko in *Great Golf Stories* records that Nelson was an incredibly straight hitter. He hit "frozen ropes," the ball seldom moving from right-to-left in flight, or vice versa, unless he willed it so.

"He was not exceptionally long off the tee, but, like all great golfers, he had an extra fifteen yards on call when he needed it."

That reference took me back those thirty-five years to the day when I followed the threesome of Byron Nelson, Jules Huot, and Bob Grey, Jr.

Jules Huot and Bob Grey were two of Canada's finest professional golfers: Huot, a short, dapper French-Canadian from Laval-sur-le-Lac in Montreal, and Grey, a tall and handsome pro from Toronto's Scarborough Golf Club.

The two Canadians were tournament tested and, while not intimidated by Lord Byron, there is no question that they felt his presence. Both could move the ball, and on this day, it appeared, they had let out a little shaft. For several holes they had out-driven Nelson, but he appeared oblivious to the challenge. That is, he ignored the challenge of the brash Canadians until it became obvious, from reaction and applause from the gallery, that the crowd thought the three were having a driving competition — and that the Canadians were winning.

This all came back to me as I read Al Burko's comment about Nelson's having an extra fifteen yards on call when he needed it. Make that fifty yards, Al.

Here's what happened. By this time the juices were really flowing for little Jules Huot and, on a particularly long par-five hole, he sent a screamer down the centre of the fairway.

Bob Grey, who was one of Canada's long-ball hitters at that time, went a full twenty yards past Huot's ball.

And then Lord Byron accepted the challenge. He did this simply by murmuring "Uh, huh," and by almost imperceptibly flexing his fingers as he gripped his driver. He also took an extra-long glance down the fairway just to be sure that the gallery got the message. His swing was as flawless as ever, but he called on that extra power that was there for the asking. His ball passed Bob Grey on the fly and appeared to be rising when it did. It was a good twenty-five yards beyond Grey and well over three hundred yards down the centre of the fairway — and that was that. It was also the end of the day's driving competition. Nelson went back to the job at hand, which, for him, was winning the tournament. Which he did.

−30−

Doug Lewis:
He Remembers the Good Times, and...

– – – – – – –
– – – – –
–

HE'S OLDER NOW, as are most of us. His once trim, twenty-eight-inch waist has expanded eight or twenty inches. His hair is thinner and he's pushing into middle age.

Once he played as many as 140 games of golf in New Brunswick's short season. Now he plays half a dozen games a year, "if you could call it playing," he says with a wry smile.

He was a champion. A club champion at the Moncton Golf club, a two-time N.B.-P.E.I. junior champion back in the early 1950s, and the N.B.-P.E.I. amateur champion in 1961. He played on a number of N.B.-P.E.I. Willingdon Cup teams in national competition, and his was a class act.

How could he give it up?

"It wasn't really my choice, not exactly," said Doug Lewis as we sat together and reminisced on a recent flight from Toronto to Saint John. "The game left me, so I left the game." When it got to the point that he couldn't break 85, the one-time Moncton perfectionist decided to spend more time at the beach with his family.

"Now I play half a dozen friendly games and enjoy myself. If I hit some good shots, I get a kick out of them. If I don't, well...."

His voice trails off, leaving the impression that he doesn't suffer on the course when things go wrong, but still there are memories of the glory days, and one day, he concedes, he may return and give it another try.

Doug Lewis came by the game honestly. His father Vic, an outstanding baseball pitcher half a century ago, has been a golf addict for as long as anyone can remember. He's seventy-two now, still plays regularly, and shot his age in Florida last winter. Doug's brother Brian was a onetime N.B.-P.E.I. junior champion, and if memory serves me well, his mother and a sister also were golfers.

Doug Lewis enjoyed playing with older players when he was working to become a champion some thirty years ago, and among those he remembers well is Ben Isner, a one-time N.B.-P.E.I. and Maritime amateur champion.

Ben, who died in 1969, always had a new theory about golf. He experimented with his swing, and several times a year he would convince himself that he finally had the game mastered.

Doug Lewis remembered driving with Ben Isner to Riverside, the site of the N.B.-P.E.I. Championship, in the early 1950s. Ben was the defending champion, and he had a lot of confidence on the trip from Moncton.

"I've finally got it," he told young Doug Lewis. He had been swinging with his woods, but punching his irons. That had created an inconsistency, but just the night before on the practice tee he had put one smooth swing together for all shots. He was ready to defend his championship. Watch out, Riverside!

But on his first round he shot an 87. Ah, well, back to the drawing board.

Doug also remembered how his own game slipped away from him. One year, when he was at the peak of his form, he recalled standing on the first tee at Riverside and wondering, "who in this field can beat me?"

Three years later he was back on the same tee, not playing the same amount of golf and wondering, "who in this field can I beat?"

Most of his memories of golf are happy ones, but not all of them. He recalls the shattering experience of being disqualified for missing his starting time by a minute and a half in his first national tournament at the Kanawaki Golf Club in Montreal in 1953. He even remembers the RCGA [Royal Canadian Golf Association] official who told him he was out of the tournament. "It was Colin Rankin, and he's the only RCGA official of that time that I remember."

Doug Lewis isn't bitter, but I got the impression that his memory of Colin Rankin is not a fond one.

Jimmy Foster, the New Brunswick RCGA governor at the time, was furious but there was nothing he could do.

It didn't help matters for either Foster or Lewis later in the tournament when Ontario amateur champion Gerry Kesselring was called for his tee-off time and sent word from the dining room that he would be out as soon as he finished his sandwich.

But the kid from the Maritimes was taught a lesson. It was a hard lesson and one he never forgot. From that day on, and as long as he participated in tournament golf, Doug Lewis was always ready to go half an hour before his tee-off time.

But if that is an unhappy memory, Doug Lewis has more than his share of good memories and warm thoughts about the game and the people who play it.

One of his great thrills came in 1956 when the Canadian amateur championship was played at the Edmundston Golf Club. "I was hitting three-woods to my caddy on the practice fairway and Moe Norman came over, told his caddy to go out by mine, and started hitting an iron beyond my wood shots — but he was hitting a seven-iron."

What did Doug Lewis do?

"I called my caddy in and joined the gallery watching Norman."

Norman, one of the living legends of Canadian golf, won his second straight amateur championship at Edmundston and later turned pro. He still shoots par and sub-par golf.

Another practice tee incident stands out among Doug Lewis's golf memories. The year was 1961 and he had won the N.B.-P.E.I. amateur championship. He was in Edmonton for the Canadian amateur championship when someone came into the clubhouse at the Edmonton Golf Club and told the golfers they should go down to the practice tee to see a big American smashing irons out of sight.

Doug followed a group to the practice tee, where a huge man, a member of the US Ryder Cup team, which had been invited to compete in the amateur championship, was hitting long irons. "I'd never seen anyone hit an iron with such power," he recalled.

"Who is he?" Doug asked someone in the gallery. "Some amateur from the US," he was told. "His name is Jack Nicklaus."

That was the year Jack Nicklaus won his second US amateur championship. The next year Jack Nicklaus — as a professional — won his first US Open championship and started his march through the history pages of golf.

−30−

SOME GOOD BOOKS

Growing Up: Russell Baker's Story of the Depression Years

‒ ‒ ‒ ‒ ‒ ‒ ‒
‒ ‒ ‒ ‒ ‒
‒

ONE OF THE FINEST BOOKS published in 1982 was Russell Baker's story of growing up. Russell Baker is an award-winning columnist of the *New York Times* and that was the name of the book — *Growing Up*.

It is a compelling story, a sad and funny story. It contains tragedy and bitterness, humour, laughter, and heartache. If you lived through the Depression Years, you are taken back in a magic time capsule to visit once again a time that will never be fully understood by those who did not experience it.

Russell Baker takes you back to your childhood, back to the time when families faced adversity together, shared what little they had, back to a period when proud families believed accepting government handouts was a disgrace, not a right. It was a time in our history when selling the *Saturday Evening Post* at five cents a copy made Russell Baker the family's most important money earner.

I'd recommend *Growing Up* to anyone who grew up in the Depression except for one small flaw — the Pulitzer Prize-winning Baker, you see, stole every word in the book.

It is a case of out-and-out plagiarism.

This is not, as it purports to be, the story of Russell Baker growing up in the backwoods of Virginia, later in a small town in New Jersey, and still later in Depression-racked, jobless Baltimore.

It is the story of my brother Doug Costello growing up in Saint John.

Doug, who started his own career in journalism as a sports writer on the *Telegraph-Journal*, retired late last year at sixty-six and has retreated to Kennebunk in Maine, where he can sit in a rocking chair and admire his many writing and editing awards gathered while editor of the *Aroostook Republican* in Maine and later the *Pottsville Republican* in Pennsylvania.

Except that Doug Costello isn't quite ready for a rocking chair. Not yet. He is still too busy writing to think of sitting in a rocking chair, let alone sitting and rocking.

But I suspect he has more time on his hands than I, so I've advised him to sue Baker.

The *New York Times'* internationally respected writer and editor Harrison Salisbury described the book as the saddest, funniest, most comical picture of coming of age in the United States in the Depression Years and World War II that has ever been written.

It is all of those things, but it just isn't Russell Baker. It is Doug Costello, and if you want to know, it is a little of Ralph Costello, too.

Come to think of it, you are likely to find yourself in this book of haunting memories, this story of America beaten and driven to her knees, and of the people who lived each day with disaster but somehow muddled through and managed to survive.

Russell Baker recalls his own unenthusiastic and timid efforts to sell the *Saturday Evening Post* and later the *Baltimore News-Post* and the *Sunday American*, and how his young sister Doris, then seven years of age, took over the street corner sales of the *Saturday Evening Post* with such zest that she sold every copy within a matter of minutes.

Her approach was very simple and very direct. When the light turned red, she would stride to the nearest car and bang her small fist on the window. When the driver, probably thinking his car was being attacked by a midget, lowered the window, she would thrust the magazine in his face and tell him he needed a magazine. "It only costs a nickel."

It worked, according to Baker.

Well, it may have worked, but it didn't happen in the New Jersey community of Belleville as he claims. It took place in Saint John at the corner of Princess and Prince William Streets.

Doug Costello was eleven and he was the newsboy. At six, I was his helper. He was either timid and reluctant or just plain smart. In any event, he would stand in the background while a frail six-year-old confronted the businessmen with shouts of "Get your paper . . . read all about it." And even in the Depression years, the most cold-hearted businessman, buying a two-cent newspaper, didn't often have the nerve to wait for change for a nickel while I fumbled about looking for change that never seemed to come out of my pocket. We were a good selling team, Doug and I, and it hurts when someone steals our story, changes the locale, makes a six-year-old boy a seven-year-old girl—and wins a Pulitzer Prize. That's why I think Doug should sue.

Oh, I wouldn't mind too much if it were only the newsboy story, but Russell Baker stole much more than that.

Somehow Baker must have learned how Doug and I used to listen to the radio broadcasts of Joe Louis fights in our second-storey bedroom on Charles Street. This was in the 1930s, when, as Baker recounted, the crackling voice of Clem McCarthy would tell us fight after fight, "Louis measures him, a left to the jaw, a right to the body . . . ." And then it was all over.

Somehow, in some mysterious, unexplainable way, Baker also learned of how proud the Saint John black community was in those days when the Brown Bomber was the king of the heavyweights.

They were proud of Louis's record and they were proud of their own athletic accomplishments, and they had good reason.

In Saint John during the 1930s and into the '40s we had many outstanding black athletes—among them Ossie and Billy Stewart, two talented and exciting speed skaters; Nick Skinner, the track-and-field speedster; Elmer Sadleir and Dumb Edison, basketball stars.

Dumb Edison? Yes, that's what we called him then. I wouldn't do it now, but it seemed proper enough when we were growing up. Dumb Edison was a big, raw-boned athlete who played basketball in the South End. He was anything but dumb when he cut for the basket, and if you were in the way that was your misfortune.

It was just as natural to call him Dumb Edison as it was to know other athletes as Rip Seely, Fat Badger, Wild Bill MacDonald, Billy (The Kid) Thome, and Killer Ken Vallis. Vallis wasn't a killer and Edison wasn't dumb, but most athletes had nicknames. Remember Aukie Titus and Bush Nickerson and Twinkle Toes

Sammy McManus? How about Moose LeBlanc? Who would ever forget how the crowd at the Forum would rise when Vince Livingston in his later years as a hockey player, would wind up from his defence position and start down the ice: "Rosie. Rosie. Go for it, Rosie," the crowd would scream.

But we were talking about the Saint John black community. Now, obviously it wouldn't make much sense for Russell Baker to tell the story of Doug and Ralph Costello listening to Joe Louis fights and the Saint John black community strutting about town when Louis was on a winning streak, which was just about all the time in the 1930s.

So Baker has changed the scene to Baltimore, where he is supposed to be the young boy listening to the radio. It is Louis's second fight with Max Schmeling, the German white hope. Schmeling had not only defeated Louis in the first fight, he had knocked him out. Here's how Baker tells what happened: "At the bell Louis left his corner, appraised Schmeling the way a butcher eyes a side of beef — then punched him senseless in two minutes and nine seconds."

Baker then describes how the blacks of Baltimore came out of the city that traditionally had been their place, their own neighbourhood, how they marched and strutted proudly out of Lemmon Street and into the white areas of the community.

"Joe Louis had given them the courage to assert their right to use a public thoroughfare, and there wasn't a white person down there to dispute it. It was the first civil rights demonstration I ever saw, and it was completely spontaneous, ignited by the finality with which Joe Louis had destroyed the theory of white superiority."

Fine. That's the way it was in those days, back in the 1930s when Joe Louis gave new pride to his race. This was long before Jackie Robinson broke the baseball colour bar with the Brooklyn Dodgers and long before blacks took over basketball and the domination of practically any sport in which they care to compete.

But the person Baker describes as a young boy listening to the radio is Doug Costello, and the blacks who walked proudly were the blacks of Saint John — because of their own accomplishments as athletes and because of the man who had destroyed Hitler's myth of white supremacy.

It happened in Saint John, Mr. Baker. Saint John, not Baltimore.

And that's why I've told Doug he should sue.

But even if, on the evidence so far, you are not prepared to believe that Baker somehow stole Doug Costello's life story, there is yet more convincing evidence. Irrefutable evidence.

In one section of his book, Russell Baker boasts about being able to make a typewriter rattle like a machine gun.

This, believe me, was Doug Costello's trademark.

Anyone who worked in the 1940s in the old newsroom on Canterbury Street, or anyone who visited the newsroom in the evenings while the work was in progress, will remember the machine-gun production of the typewriters—and the fastest, loudest, machine-gun delivery was from the typewriter of sports writer Doug Costello.

His trademark was a warm-up of about ten seconds as he pounded the right elevation key with his little finger, and then the stories would pour forth—the old iron-framed Underwood spitting out the words like a machine gun.

So, you see, it was Doug Costello, not Russell Baker, who originated and perfected the machine-gun typing style.

Ask Jimmy O'Sullivan, now a vice-president at the University of New Brunswick. Ask Hal Wood, the editor of the *Daily Gleaner*, or Scott Webster of the New Brunswick Power Commission, or a dozen others. Ask Don Smith, who could beat a mean typewriter himself in those days and still knocks out a weekly report for the *Kings County Record*. Ask Jack Warner, now a lawyer in Fredericton but then a school teacher by day who worked nights at the *Telegraph-Journal* and studied law in his spare time. They'll remember who had a machine gun for a typewriter. It wasn't Russell Baker. It was Doug Costello.

Among other things, the Russell Baker account of *Growing Up* is a heart-warming and heart-tearing story, as old as history itself, of two fiercely competitive women seeking the love and affection of a young child caught in the age-old struggle between a mother-in-law who wants nothing to do with the mother but craves with all her heart and all her being for the attention, the affection, and the love, especially the love, of the favourite grandchild.

Russell Baker takes you to the heart of that struggle as he tells of the battle fought so bitterly, with words and looks and guile. It is the story of the grandmother who sought to buy young Russell's love, with anything and everything at her disposal.

Here is a passage from *Growing Up* that captures the seething rage and hatred between Baker's mother and his grandmother:

> My grandmother thought my mother kept me under too much discipline and delighted in taking me to her cellar pantry and stuffing me with forbidden treats. One afternoon she took me down there in the darkness to feed me on her homemade bread. Slicing a thick piece for each of us, she laid on a coat of butter, then said, "You want jelly on top of it?" "Yes ma'am, please."
>
> She took a jar from the shelf and removed the wax and had the knife poised to plunge in when we were caught. "Russell, what're you doing back in there?" My mother was silhouetted in the doorway.
>
> "Grandma's fixing me a piece of jelly bread." My mother spoke to Ida Rebecca. "You know I don't want him eating between meals." Her voice was terrible with anger.
>
> So was Ida Rebecca's. "Are you going to tell me how to raise a boy?"
>
> "I'm telling you I don't want him eating jelly bread between meals. He's my child, and he'll do as I tell him."
>
> "Don't you come in here telling me how to raise children. I raised a dozen children, and not one of them ever dared raise their voice to me like you do."
>
> I cowered between them while the shouting rose, but they had forgotten me now as the accumulated bitterness spewed out of them. Finally, my mother noticed I was still standing there with the buttered bread in my hand. "I want you to stay on the other side of the road where you belong," she said to me.
>
> "He belongs over here just as much as he belongs over there," my grandmother exclaimed.
>
> The anger seemed to drain suddenly out of my mother. She started to leave but turned at the door and said, very much in control of her temper, "You can eat the buttered bread, but I don't

want any jelly put on it." At this Ida Rebecca jabbed her knife into the jar and smeared the bread with a thick coat of jelly, all the time glaring at my mother. "Eat it," she commanded.

I waited until my mother marched out, very near tears, I judged, and then I ate it while Ida Rebecca watched. I didn't dare not to.

Only that did not happen, as Russell Baker claims it did, in the backwoods of Virginia. It happened in a large, grey building on Prince Edward Street across from the cotton mill, where Grandmother Costello and my mother conducted the old, sometimes wordless, tight-lipped struggle for the affection of my brother Doug in the 1920s and into the 1930s.

Doug was the first grandchild, but he was more than that. He was born on November 16, Grandmother Costello's own birthday. He was a darkly beautiful child, with curly hair and an almost angelic face when he was young (that is, when he was very young). He was the favourite of his grandparents.

He was bribed by his grandmother — as was I, but to a lesser degree — bribed with fruit, with candy, money for the movies, with clothes, and, in her own way, with love.

The grandchildren were loved, the mother tolerated, or less. The mother, a Protestant who had joined the Roman Catholic Church when she married my father, was already suspect. Some day, Grandmother Costello believed, this intruder would break away from the Church and take the children with her. My grandmother was right, and this is why there are so many Baptist Costellos around these days.

But what galls me is that Russell Baker has stolen this, our family story. He has changed the names and the location, and he has written one of the most moving accounts ever recorded of growing up in the Depression. That story, our story, won him a Pulitzer Prize. It probably made him a million dollars.

That's why I want my brother Doug to sue.

I also want you to read Russell Baker's book.

I want you to read *Growing Up* because, if you lived through the Depression, you will find that Russell Baker also stole a page or a chapter from your life. This is not simply the story of Russell Baker growing up, it is the story of the Depression—the story of growing up between two World Wars, it is the story of dreams and hopes and laughter and, in so many ways, it is a story of raw courage.

It is a classic of our times that could have had its setting in any community, large or small, anywhere in the United States or Canada. It is pure history, written with the haunting touch of a master storyteller. It is the story of Russell Baker's life, and Doug Costello's, and yours, and mine.

−30−

Alden Nowlan:
What Made His Writing So Special

— — — — — — —
— — — — —
—

IT MUST HAVE BEEN TWENTY-FIVE YEARS since that night when I sat next to Fred Cogswell at a dinner party given by Lord Beaverbrook at the University of New Brunswick during one of his fall visits to New Brunswick.

It was one of those invigorating nights when Lord Beaverbrook was at his mischievous best. His target that night was Brigadier Michael Wardell, then publisher of the *Daily Gleaner* and a long-time Beaverbrook associate dating back to their days together on the *Express*, when that newspaper was one of the glittering lights of Fleet Street journalism.

Lord Beaverbrook held Wardell in some considerable affection, but he loved to needle the man. Among other things, he would do this by referring to the brigadier as The Corporal. Lord Beaverbrook would smile wickedly when he did so; Wardell would also smile, but not with much enthusiasm, and in fact on these occasions Wardell's response was much closer to a painful grimace than a smile.

So it was one of those nights to be remembered — a night of excellent food and wine, stimulating conversation, and a lot of attention for Lord Beaverbrook, who did not at all mind performing his role with wit and grace, not to mention occasional discomfort to Brigadier Wardell.

And that is probably what I would have remembered of it—if it hadn't been for Fred Cogswell.

I knew Fred Cogswell by name and reputation, but I believe that was the first time I had met him. He was an English professor at UNB and a poet, and in many ways the guiding light and inspiration of many young Canadian poets who first had their work published in the *Fiddlehead*, a publication that he alone was largely responsible for maintaining.

Fred Cogswell kept bending my ear that night about a young reporter at the *Hartland Observer*. That reporter was also a poet—"the best young poet in Canada today," said Fred Cogswell.

The poet's name was Alden Nowlan.

The message finally got through and it has stayed with me ever since.

Later, Alden Nowlan was to come to Saint John to work as a reporter and news editor of the *Telegraph-Journal*. He was everything Fred Cogswell said, and more.

In the twenty years since Alden Nowlan came down from Hartland to join the *Telegraph-Journal*, his name, his style, and his views have graced the columns of this newspaper—and it has been a much better newspaper because of his contributions.

Those were active years and gratifying years for the pen of Alden Nowlan. They were the years in which he built a national reputation as a writer, poet, novelist, and playwright.

He won countless awards, he joined with gifted artist Tom Forrestall in the publication of an outstanding volume of paintings and poetry, and later, in partnership with Walter Learning, he turned out numerous successful plays for stage, radio, and television.

Throughout this extremely busy period, he continued a weekly column for the *Telegraph-Journal*, and regular articles for other publications.

In this newspaper his Saturday columns were looked forward to eagerly by thousands of readers. He wrote with humour, warmth, and perception. Often he moved his readers to tears or the threshold of tears.

It is difficult to single out any one column, but there is one I will refer to. It was one of the columns in which Alden Nowlan, a child of the Depression, recalled and revealed the love he had for his father—without ever saying it quite that way — and the appreciation and understanding he had for the adults of the Depression who suffered so much not because of their inability to provide for themselves, but because of their inability to provide for their children.

It was a story of pure love, and I am going to quote a few paragraphs from it because this is the Alden Nowlan whose memory brought the past so vividly to light, the Alden Nowlan of such unusual and deep and loving perception.

Here are some excerpts from that column:

> Christmas morning is one time in the year when I feel sorry for the kids of today.
>
> They have so much, there are so many things they take for granted. I'm not saying that's bad. In lots of ways they're luckier than the kids of my generation.
>
> But, there's certainly not much left for them to get excited about at Christmas.
>
> A 10-speed bicycle might do it. But not always. The kid with a 10-speed will be looking for a moped.
>
> The kids of my generation shivered in anticipation over a single orange. Did I say a single orange? We shivered in anticipation over a single grape.
>
> No, no, no, we weren't starving. In some ways we sons and daughters of the Great Depression were better fed than the scions of the Affluent Society. There was no junk food in those days.
>
> But there were certain things — oranges, grapes, nuts and candies — that we tasted only at Christmas.
>
> I still stock up on oranges, grapes, nuts and ribbon candy at Christmas. But it's not the same. And it isn't just that I'm now grown-up. The difference is that I can have any of those things at any time I want them.
>
> I've never tasted anything better than those grapes, those oranges, those walnuts, almonds, filberts, pecans, and brazils, that ribbon candy, those candy canes.
>
> There was one kind of candy that we didn't like as much as the others. Barley toys, I think they were called.

That was the only kind my father would accept. When I was
a little kid I thought that was because he liked it best. Adults have
strange tastes, after all.

Now, of course, I realize that he didn't like barley toys any
more than we did. But if he had eaten any of the candies we liked
he'd have felt that he was taking something away from us.

A very small sacrifice, true. But one that makes me smile,
lovingly, at the memory of it. The only Christmas gift that
the man received was that one barley toy that he'd bought
himself — that, and the expression on his children's faces.

That vignette from the early life of Alden Nowlan reveals something of the
power of his writing.

And what joy those lines would have brought to Alden's father if he could
have lived to read them. His father, who also died young, was never embraced
by the warmth of those loving words written by his son — but here is part of
what was so special about Alden Nowlan's writing: other fathers and other sons
would read those lines and would remember similar events in their lives, and
they would treasure their own memories, and the world would be a better place
for it all. Just as, in some small way, this world is a better place because Alden
Nowlan visited it. All too briefly.

–30–

Alden Nowlan's Love-in: They Called It a Funeral

IT WAS THE KIND OF A FUNERAL Alden Nowlan would have appreciated—if only he hadn't been the corpse.

But there was no changing that. He'd bought the farm, as they say up in Carleton County, and Alden was as dead as he was ever going to be, so those who loved him in life had a Nowlan love-in and they called it a funeral.

Alden Nowlan would have approved.

There was a lot of hugging at Alden's funeral. Not those fleeting, touch-the-cheeks and pat-on-the-back hugs, but real, honest-to-goodness Alden Nowlan bear hugs—the kind that tells you someone cares, as Alden Nowlan cared about the people he loved and his fellow man for all the years he lived on this earth.

There were some tears, but not too many. Most everyone was pretty well cried out by the time of the funeral. Inevitably, there were some smiles as Alden's friends recalled incidents from the life they had shared with him. Yes, and there was laughter.

There was laughter because the people closest to Alden Nowlan were happy, stimulating, creative people; they had sat and talked and drunk and laughed with him while he was alive, and he would not forgive them if they changed because he was gone.

No, let there be no doubt. This was the funeral that Alden Nowlan would have wanted. It was a love-in funeral arranged with meticulous detail by his son Johnny.

And when it was all over someone said, "You did good, Johnny. You did good." Not the language as written by Alden Nowlan, but there was no mistaking the message. It could not have been said with greater clarity or meaning. "You did good, Johnny. You did good."

Alden, the boy from the wrong side of the tracks who grew up in the grim Depression Years and carved a place for himself in Canadian letters in the fifty short years he was given on this earth, would have agreed. And, grammar aside, he too would have said, "You did good, Johnny, You did good."

Alden would have approved the simple setting and the small private group that gathered in the chapel of the old Arts Building at UNB to hear tributes from Walter Learning, Premier Richard Hatfield, and Jamie Stewart.

He would have been pleased by the presence of old friend Bob Tweedie and touched if he could have heard Tweedie asking the unanswerable question: "Why is a young and gifted man like Alden taken away and someone like me left to occupy space when I've already had my full run?" Bob Tweedie shook his head sadly. "There isn't any answer," he said. And there isn't.

Walter Learning, Alden's collaborator in so many successful writing ventures, flew in from Vancouver to bid his friend and colleague farewell in a tribute that touched on Alden's great contribution to writing in Canada, his love for humanity, and especially his love for his wife Claudine and son Johnny.

Similar words came from Premier Hatfield, whose friendship with Nowlan goes back to the time of Alden's arrival in Hartland to work as a young reporter for Charlie Allan, publisher of the *Hartland Observer*. Over the years Hatfield had been reminded by Nowlan's writing of the small community in which he grew up. He also had been impressed and moved by the strength of the bonds of the family.

Jamie Stewart used a prized flute, "one of the most simple of musical instruments," to play an Irish lament at the chapel. When he finished he broke the flute over his right knee. It had played at Alden Nowlan's funeral. It would never be heard again.

Alden would have been touched by that gesture as he would have been moved by the presence of Aida Flemming, widow of former Premier Hugh John Flemming, and by Fred Cogswell and others.

The pallbearers were his son John Nowlan, Jamie Stewart and David Adams Richards, who also were like sons to Alden, who had a capacity for making those he loved part of his family. Other pallbearers were Jon Pederson, John Orser, Robert Gibbs, Michael Brian Oliver, and Walter Learning.

The bagpipes played, and Walter Learning read one of Alden's poems at the graveside on a beautiful rise at Forest Hill Cemetery, and it might have been any other funeral. Except that it wasn't.

Alden Nowlan was not going on his final journey without a proper toast from his friends, nor while his son was alive and breathing—so a bottle of Jameson's finest was produced and a loving cup went the rounds of the pallbearers before Johnny sent the bottle itself crashing into the coffin, which had just been lowered into the grave.

With that, Johnny's coat was flung to the ground and he picked up a shovel. Strangers would not bury his father.

And that is why on a warm June afternoon three gravediggers stood in the background and watched bemused as Johnny Nowlan and soon all the pallbearers, and others in the funeral party, shovelled dirt into the grave of Alden Nowlan, writer, poet, and humanist, dead at fifty.

When Alden Nowlan's stone is erected, it will be butting against that of famous New Brunswick poet Bliss Carman. A fit resting place for one of the enormous talents of our time.

And if we had listened carefully on that beautiful afternoon earlier this week, we might well have heard a gruff but loving voice wafting gently through the trees at Forest Hill Cemetery, and it would have been saying, "You did good, Johnny. You did good."

−30−

Lobsters: A Dirty Book by a Dirty Old Man

_— — — — — — —_
_— — — — —_
_—_

AWAY BACK IN HISTORY, back in the Middle Ages—why, back more than twenty-five years ago—Stuart Trueman decided he would write a book. He called it _Cousin Elva_. It was a successful first novel even if most of the stories were thinly disguised incidents adapted from his own very real and very unusual life. The book sold well and was made into a television program. Reprints followed and so did other books.

I would like to say that Stuart Trueman has not looked back since the publication of his first book, but that would not be true. Stuart Trueman is forever looking back over his shoulder, through his legs, by using a mirror. Like baseball's legendary Satchel Paige, he wants to be sure that nothing is gaining on him.

But even if he does look back, furtively and often, even if he goes through life expecting the bubble to burst at any moment, he has continued to write books that bring happiness and joy to his many loyal readers. He also writes a weekly column for this newspaper, makes numerous public appearances as an after-dinner speaker, and serves as an unofficial goodwill ambassador for New Brunswick. He has in fact been writing books full-time for the last eleven years, ever since he had the good sense to retire after forty-two years with this newspaper, the last twenty as editor.

He is back in Florida now, sitting in the sun, no doubt, and worrying about his New Brunswick friends, who must look forward to a winter of ice, snow, and sleet. I am sure this makes him very unhappy.

It was just before he left on his trip south that I realized he is seventy-one (I realized this the moment he told me he was celebrating his seventy-first birthday). After mentioning rather casually that it was his birthday ("This is my birthday, I'm seventy-one today."), he just stood there in front of my desk until I realized he was waiting for me to say something. Happy Birthday didn't seem quite appropriate, so to cheer him up I said, "I never thought you'd make it."

I think that cheered him up, but with Stu it is hard to tell. He is only happy when he has something to be unhappy about.

Happy or unhappy, he does bring joy and happiness to others with a sense of humour that sustained him through the Depression Years and a great many years since. He remains extremely active, prolific, entertaining, informative, and amusing — not to mention cautious, wary, uncertain, suspicious, and frustrated.

All of these many moods will be apparent to his countless followers when they read his latest book, *Don't Let Them Smell the Lobsters Cooking.*

His is a self-deprecating sense of humour, and it is as fresh and lively today at seventy-one as it was more than half a century ago when he started his career as a young reporter and cartoonist. Stu Trueman has spent a lifetime laughing at himself and sharing his laughter with the world. He would have you believe that he is the biggest joke of all — and in a way he's right. Who else sits on a freshly painted toilet seat, gets stuck, and has to extricate himself one painful hair at a time?

Who else blows his top because his wife has the audacity to tell him to be careful not to get on the wrong plane at an airport, becomes so upset that he dashes off in a huff and gets on the wrong plane — and doesn't learn of it until he reaches the wrong destination, which also happens to be the termination of the flight?

Yes, Stuart Trueman is a funny man. A funny man of letters, a funny man to laugh with, and very often, because he makes himself the brunt of his own jokes, a funny man to laugh at.

It is a pleasure to read his books and a pleasure to review them, which I am about to do. This review will be in three parts for reasons that may or may not become obvious, according to the reading skills and general intelligence of the readers. Here goes.

Part one: it is a dirty book by a dirty old man. There is no other way to describe it.

Stuart Trueman talks about lobsters, but that is just to get the book past the censors, to make sure he doesn't end up in court on an obscenity charge.

He obviously hopes that all his talk about lobsters and the smell of lobsters will camouflage his obsession with crotchless panties, the wedding-night scene when he ripped his wife's satin nightie to shreds, the night he cavorted bottomless in a hotel corridor, the story of the middle-aged housewives charged with hooking in Mexico City, the revelation of his own mother's innocent indiscretion when she was mistaken for a local madam by foreign sailors, the businessman arguing the price of services with Las Vegas hookers, a visit to Minnie Eaton's Golden Grove emporium of pleasure, and so it goes. Is Stuart Trueman the writer of this? Yes. Is it a dirty book? Yes.

It is an unusual selection of bathroom humour and worse by a gifted author who kept on the straight and narrow for the first seventy years of his life — and then went sadly astray in the book published to coincide with his seventy-first birthday.

If you want a dirty book, buy *Lobsters*. You won't be disappointed.

Part two: it's a love story. Pure and simple. A truly beautiful love story. Stuart Trueman didn't intend it to be a love story. He thought he was writing humour, but the love comes through on almost every page.

Stuart Trueman worried when he wrote the chapter about his mother. She was a strong-willed woman, something of an eccentric, perhaps at times a character. The author paints a clear and accurate picture of his mother in the chapter entitled "My Unusual Mother." His stories of his mother are so vivid that he thought they might offend her memory. He need not have worried. His appreciation and love for his unusual mother are subtle but overpowering for any perceptive reader.

He didn't use these exact words, but the chapter really says one thing: "I Love You, Mama." He remembers the last words she said to him, shortly before she died, but I've already given away too much. You'll have to buy the book if you want to share this remarkable love story.

The book is a love story in other ways, too. His affection for his sons, Douglas and Mac, comes through strongly, and there are the warm stories when he was courting Mildred Stiles at the Stiles farm in Albert County. Why, this man even appears to have loved his mother-in-law and perhaps his grandmother-in-law, Grandma Colpitts.

His recollections are warm and tender. Stuart Trueman thought he was writing a funny book, but it turned out to be a love story.

Part three: in some ways, and perhaps in many ways, this is the best book he has ever written. It contains so much information, so many memories, so many names, incidents, and anecdotes. It has more laughter, love, and charm than any of his other books, and I've read them all from his start more than a quarter of a century ago with *Cousin Elva*.

It is a book that should be in every home. It is about the people of New Brunswick, the people who live in Saint John, those who grew up by the sea, on farms. It is a trip behind the scenes into the newsrooms of the old newspapers of New Brunswick in the days of the Dirty Thirties.

If you are over fifty and a New Brunswicker, it is mandatory reading. If you are under fifty, it is one of the best history books to be written about New Brunswick, covering the time period from the turn of the century to the present. The Department of Education should see that it is in every school in New Brunswick. Why not a history book that young people will read, enjoy, and learn from? I recommend it highly.

−30−

Stuart Trueman: "The Devil Made Me Do It"

———————
—————
—

"IT ISN'T GOING to work, Stu."

"What isn't going to work?" Stuart Trueman tried to look innocent, but that didn't work either. He's guilty as sin and he knows it.

"Don't play that innocent game with me," I said. "I know what you're up to."

Stuart Trueman, writer, editor, author, historian, raconteur, had just handed me a copy of his new book, which is entitled *Life's Odd Moments*.

I'd flipped through several pages while he stood there, on the other side of my desk, waiting eagerly for a favourable reaction.

I closed the book and threw it on the floor in disgust.

"Does this mean you don't like it?" he asked.

"No," I said, "that means I love it. I always throw books on the floor when I like them. If I don't like them I throw them out the window."

"Is it the illustrations?" Stu asked.

"What?"

"The illustrations. I did my own illustrations this time. Don't you like the drawings?"

"It isn't the illustrations."

"Then it's the cover."

"What?"

"The cover. I didn't do the cover. The cover design was done by Marie Bartholomew. I knew she'd ruin it with the cover. It was the raccoon, wasn't it? They shouldn't have put a raccoon on the cover; that will drive people away. It was the cover you didn't like, wasn't it?"

"The cover's all right."

"Then what is it? Why did you throw the book on the floor?"

"Because," I paused to measure each word carefully, "because," I repeated, "you're jealous of Mildred's success and you've written another dirty book in desperation." This was a reference to his thinly disguised book about lobsters, which were, in fact, not lobsters but ladies of the night. "But it isn't going to work. You can't peddle that kind of trash in New Brunswick."

Stuart Trueman is old. He's on the wrong side of seventy and he's aged ten years in the last twelve months. It's nothing physical. It's just that he can't stand his wife Mildred's success. He's been a writer all his life. Most of the time he's been an overweight writer, thanks to his wife's prowess in the kitchen. But last year, finally fed up with the role of a docile homemaker and wife of New Brunswick's best-known author, Mildred came out of the kitchen with a book of her own.

It was called *Favourite Recipes from Old New Brunswick Kitchens* and when Stu brought me a copy I took one glance and said, "It's a natural. I'll bet it outsells anything you've ever written."

I remember Stu's reaction. It was a smirk. A condescending smirk. It wasn't a particularly nice smirk because, among other things, Stuart Trueman isn't all that good at smirking, he doesn't have much to smirk about, so he doesn't get very much practice. But on that occasion he smirked as he said, "Oh it'll probably sell a few copies, and it gave her something to do."

The rest is history. Mildred's book became a bestseller. It's still ringing the cash registers of New Brunswick's book stores, and it's long since outsold Stu's best seller.

All of this has been very trying for Stuart Trueman, who managed to keep the real talent in the family confined to the kitchen for about fifty years. He likes to see the royalties rolling in, but he hates being relegated to the role of Second Banana.

At cocktail parties he cringes and goes into a silent sulk when he is asked if he is the husband of Mildred Trueman, the author.

"I didn't think anyone would notice," Stu said.

"You didn't think anyone would notice? You didn't think anyone would notice? Don't give me that line, Stu. It was deliberate: you're trying to get back on the bestseller list by using obscene gutter language. You should be writing for *Playboy* and *Hustler*."

"I didn't think it was that bad."

"'Not that bad.' Not that bad? Why, you've got words in this book that would make Richard Nixon blush."

"They made me do it," he sobbed. "I had no option. The editors made me do it."

"They made you do it?" They made you use those words?"

"Yes, they're all women editors now and they all use swear words. They wouldn't let me use those dots and xs and dashes and exclamation marks. They said life is raw and if I was going to write about life I had to use raw language. The language of the streets. They made me do it."

"Don't give me that old 'The Devil Made Me Do It,' excuse, Stu. You're the author. Your name's on the book.

"Look at this," I said, flipping the book over to page 90. "Why did you have to write about those poor old men in the hospital, wetting the bed and swearing at the nurses because they thought the water pipes had burst in their room?"

"They made me do it," he repeated. "I had no option."

"Oh, you had an option all right." I kept my voice under perfect control, modulating each word carefully and clearly.

"You had an option, Stu," I said, pointing an accusing finger at his chest. "You had an option all right. You could have done the honourable thing. You could have said No. You could have refused to use that language, but you were blinded by jealously and greed."

"I couldn't help myself . . . I had no option."

"Stu, I've heard that line before, somewhere, sometime. I just can't remember when, but I do remember one thing."

"What's that?"

"It is not a line people will believe."

A TOUCH OF WHIMSY

Teng and Nixon in the White House

- - - - - - -
- - - - -
-

"HOW," RICHARD NIXON WANTED to know, "did you get back in the saddle?"

Teng Hsiao-ping pondered the question. His eyes were two inscrutable slits. They stared at and through Richard Nixon.

It was a memorable moment. Here were two of the world's most famous outcasts — Richard Nixon, the disgraced one-time president of the United States, and Teng Hsiao-ping, the twice-purged Chinese leader.

Nixon, who is credited with having started the US dialogue with communist China back in 1972, was an invited guest at the White House; Teng, the guest of honour. Nixon was still on the outs in the United States, but Teng was once again back in power, the virtual leader of a country of one billion people.

"How," Richard Nixon repeated himself, "did you get back in the saddle?"

Teng: "What did he say?"

Interpreter: "He wants to know how you got back on your horse?"

Teng: "Tell him about the old Chinese proverb: If you fall off your horse, pick yourself up, dust yourself off, start all over again."

Interpreter gives message to Nixon in Cantonese dialect. Nixon, thinking interpreter is trying to sing: "You're out of tune."

Teng: "What did he say?"

Interpreter: "He says you're out of tune."

Teng: "Tell him at least I've got my key to the executive washroom."

Nixon: "What did he say?"

Interpreter: "He said to tell you about the executive washroom."

Nixon: "It's at the head of the stairs, but they took my key away."

Interpreter: "That's Mr. Teng's point. He's got his key and you haven't got yours."

Nixon: "No, that's my point — that's what I want to know: how did he get back in the saddle?"

Teng: "What did he say?"

Interpreter: "I think he wants to know if you came here by horse?"

Teng: "Tell him we acknowledge that technologically we are a backward nation, but not that backward. We came by air and in a long black vehicle."

Nixon: "Holy Expletive Deleted! The old air-strike-and-take-them-to-the-cemetery-in-the-hearse-trick. I should have known." [Excited now] "But how did he get back in the Big House twice?"

Interpreter: "The Big House?"

Nixon: "Sure, the Big House. The White House. Or, over there, The Great Hall of the People."

Interpreter repeats question.

Teng: "I kept my key, and when the mood of the people changed, I just walked back in. There was nothing to it."

Nixon: "But why did their mood change. That's the important thing."

Teng: "I had a friend put up a sign."

Nixon: "That's all? One lousy, expletive-deleted sign?"

Teng: "No, not just any old sign. There has to be a message. Well, after I got back the first time I said there should always be a second chance for those who made mistakes, but acknowledged their mistakes, repented and learned from the error of their ways."

Nixon: "But how about the second time — you know, when they sent you back to shovel more night soil on the farms?"

Teng: "When I was out the second time I said how about the second chance I mentioned the first time."

Nixon: "Well, I'll be a horse's expletive-deleted! As simple as that!"

Teng: "You've got to have a message the people will believe."

Nixon: "That's my problem. The media distort everything I say. How did you get your message to the people?"

Teng: "I've already told you. I had a friend who put a sign up on the wall. It said I wanted a second chance and, by the way, the Gang of Four had to go."

Nixon: "Go, go where?"

Teng: "It was their turn to gather the night soil."

Nixon: "And it worked?"

Teng: "Sure it worked, but you've got to have a good sign writer."

Nixon: "But didn't the people remember all the bad things you said, and all the things they said you said, when they were calling you a Capitalist Roader? How did you get rid of the evidence?"

Teng: "Simple. It is an old Chinese saying. It goes like this: when a tapeworm would destroy you, gnawing at your body and your heart and even your soul, it is time to take the initiative."

Nixon: "That's an old Chinese proverb?"

Teng: "Yes."

Nixon: "What does it mean?"

Teng: "The first thing you do is destroy the tapes."

—30—

How Premier Hatfield
Made His Long Lake Decision

- - - - - - -
- - - - -
-

THE SCENE IS A REMOTE lumber camp on a lake in northwestern New Brunswick, and the premier of the province, the Honourable Richard Bennett Hatfield, is meeting with members of his caucus.

Several of his ministers are nervous and perspiring heavily as they sit around the bunk house and try to make conversation. The premier seems preoccupied. He is making notes on scraps of paper. No one wants to disturb him.

"He may be composing his resignation," one of the ministers whispers to a group that has gathered in a corner. "It's either that or a poem to Princess Di," says another. There is muffled laughter and the premier glances up from the table where he is working.

Immediately, there is silence. The premier has indicated his displeasure.

Finally, one of the ministers speaks: "Mr. Premier, you have got to face up to the crisis. This has gone far enough. You have to do something, say something. You have to make a decision."

The premier speaks: "What crisis? I know of no crisis."

A backbencher steps forward and thrusts out his chin defiantly: "What crisis, what crisis? Don't you know what is going on around you? Can't you sense the unrest? Can't you hear the voice of dissent?"

"I never listen to voices. They confuse me. There is no unrest in my kingdom...ah, in my province. There is no dissent."

The premier puts his Walkman earphones back in place and whistles softly to himself.

Another minister comes forward to confront the premier. "Mr. Premier, you can't hide forever. As Joe Louis once said about his opponent before a championship fight, 'He can run, but he can't hide.' You must know there is a crisis. It's in all the newspapers."

Annoyed, the premier takes off his earphones and replies, "I don't read the newspapers."

"You don't read the newspapers?"

"Only the colour comics, and then sometimes only *Peanuts*."

"But, Mr. Premier, the news has been on radio and on all the television newscasts. You must listen to the radio and watch television. You must know what is happening in New Brunswick."

"No, I don't. I don't listen to radio and I don't watch television. I read books and do a lot of thinking."

Another member of the caucus speaks up: "But surely you know what's happening in your own province."

Premier Hatfield: "I've been away a lot. I haven't been well. For a while I couldn't even talk, and then there was that thing about a golf cart."

Backbencher: "But you're back now and you said you were going to try harder. You promised. You can't ignore what is happening. You can't bury your head in the sand."

Premier Hatfield: "That was an accident."

Backbencher: "I beg your pardon?"

"An accident. It was an accident, and I didn't actually bury my head in the sand. I just drove into a sand trap. It could have happened to anyone."

Backbencher: "In the middle of the night?"

"Of course it was night. If it had been daylight I would have seen the sand trap. I'm no dummy. Besides, I play better at night."

"You play better at night?"

"Golf. I play a better game of golf at night."

"That's impossible."

"You haven't seen my game."

By now the ministers and backbenchers have had enough. They surround the premier and shout nasty things at him. "Come on, Dick, get with it. You've got to pull yourself together and make a decision."

"Okay, okay, you're probably right. I am premier and it's up to me to decide. As members of the caucus you have a right to know where I stand."

Backbencher Keith Dow steps forward and holds up his hands for attention. "Mr. Premier, just before you make your statement, I want you to know there has been nothing personal in the things I have been saying. If you're ready to make a decision, I want you to know I'll be right behind you."

Premier Hatfield: "Well, if you don't mind, I'd just as soon not have you behind me. That's a little something I learned from Dief the Chief, but thanks anyway. Now, I've decided and I'm ready to make a statement."

Chorus of members: "Okay, Mr. Premier, what is it going to be?"

"Egg sauce."

"Egg sauce?"

Backbencher: "What are you talking about, egg sauce?"

Premier Hatfield: "On my salmon. I'll have egg sauce on my salmon. You asked me to make up my mind and I've done it. I'll have egg sauce on my salmon for dinner tonight. Some of you may prefer lemon, but I'll have egg sauce."

Members of the caucus start running from the building.

Premier Hatfield: "Hey, guys, where are you going?"

But it is too late. The members race to the lake's edge and throw themselves in.

The premier puts his Walkman earphones back in place, laughs quietly, and murmurs to himself: "And they thought I couldn't make a decision."

—30—

Trouble in River City

——————
————
—

FINANCE MINISTER ALLAN MAHER: "Mr. Premier, we've got trouble right here in River City."

Premier Frank McKenna: "River City? This isn't River City, Allan. This is Fredericton."

Maher: "River City, Mr. Premier...River City. It's just an expression—you know, from the play, *The Music Man*. You must remember Robert Preston as Professor Hill, the old con artist who sold musical instruments and band uniforms to unsuspecting parents who thought their children would grow up to be famous musicians."

McKenna: "An old con artist? Mr. Maher, we don't use that kind of language. Not in my office. Not around here. People might hear and misunderstand."

Maher: "Okay, Mr. Premier, but we still have trouble right here in River City."

McKenna: "You mean the kids are back in the pool halls instead of cruising the malls?"

Maher: "Worse."

McKenna: "Worse? You mean they're smoking cigarettes?"

Maher: "No, they can't afford cigarettes anymore."

McKenna: "That's good. They shouldn't be smoking anyway."

Maher: "I said they couldn't afford cigarettes. I didn't say they were not smoking."

McKenna: "I don't understand. How can they be smoking if they are not smoking?"

Maher: "Mr. Premier, Mr. Premier ... can we get back to the subject. I just wanted to report that we are in trouble because we haven't got any money to spend, but there is also good news because our meet-the-people project worked out just as we planned it."

McKenna: "And that's the good news?"

Maher: "Yes. Now we give them the old Geraldine Routine."

McKenna: "The Old Geraldine Routine?"

Maher: "Sure, you remember when the comedian Flip Wilson used to play the role of Geraldine and say: 'The devil made me do it.'"

McKenna: "You mean that was Flip Wilson? I always thought there were two people — Flip and Geraldine. But now you tell me Flip was Geraldine. That's amazing."

Maher: "Can we get back to this, Mr. Premier?"

McKenna: "Oh, yes, of course. You want to blame your budget on the devil. I thought we were going to blame it on the feds. What has the devil got to do with all of this? Are you sure you're all right, Allan?"

Maher: "The point, Mr. Premier, is that in this case the devil is the people. Don't you remember, Mr. Premier, when we realized we would have to cut everything in sight we decided to hold those town meetings. We would listen to the people. Then we would tell them everything we did was in response to their wishes."

McKenna: "Is that why we hold those meetings?"

Maher: "Yes, Mr. Premier, that was the reason."

McKenna: "Really? Well, I thought they were a little silly. After all, we knew what we were going to do."

Maher: "I knew, you knew, the cabinet knew — but now, don't you see, it isn't our fault."

McKenna: "It isn't? Gee, that's funny. I thought we were running the government. I thought they'd blame us when we cut back on services."

Maher: "No, Mr. Premier, that's the beauty of it all. We are only doing what the people told us to do. We have no choice. The people have spoken. Now we'll come out with a budget that will freeze the ears off a monkey in hell."

McKenna: "And you say all of it's the people's fault. Couldn't we blame some of it on Barbara Baird Filliter?"

Maher: "No, Mr. Premier. This way is better. Believe me. "

McKenna: "Okay, Allan, it's your ball game. I sure hope you know what you're doing."

Maher: "Mr. Premier, just try to remember the theme . . . the people spoke . . . we listened to the people . . . the people made us do it."

McKenna: "The people? I thought it was the devil."

Maher: "Mr. Premier, not to worry. Trust me. This is going to work. Just leave the details to me."

McKenna: "Okay, Allan, if that's the way you want it, but just remember, it's your, uh, political aspirations that are in the sling."

Maher: "Yes, and yours, too, Mr. Premier. Yours, too."

−30−

The Perils of Buying
a New Car at Midnight

– – – – – – –
– – – – –
–

"WHERE ARE YOU GOING?"

The voice was unfriendly and frigid, as cold as an ice-encrusted mountain stream in mid-winter.

Yet, for some reason, I thought it would be amusing to say "out."

So I said it. "Out." It wasn't funny.

At least, she didn't think to laugh. "What do you mean, out?"

"Out," I replied. "Out, as in not in. Out." It still wasn't funny.

"I'm going out to test drive a car," I explained.

"It's twelve o'clock."

"So?"

"Twelve o'clock as in twelve o'clock midnight. You're not going out. Not in your condition."

"What condition?"

"Your mental condition. You have to be crazy."

"Look," I said, as quietly and patiently as I could manage, "I'm going out. I've got an appointment to test drive a car. The salesperson is waiting for me."

"The salesperson?"

"Yes, the salesperson."

"The salesperson? What's this about a salesperson? You don't talk that way."

"What do you mean, I don't talk that way? I just said I'm going out to test a car, I have an appointment and I have to keep it."

"You said you had an appointment with a salesperson."

"That is right."

"You've never said salesperson in your life, so that means you are going out at midnight to meet some salesgirl. Not a salesperson, but some floozie. Am I right?"

"No, you're not right."

"It's not a salesgirl?"

"She's not a floozie."

"How do you know, and why, will you tell me, are you going out in the middle of the night to test a car?"

"Because," I said, with admirable restraint, "that is when she suggested. She says night demonstrations are better. There isn't so much traffic. She does her best work at night. She says people are more relaxed and that's when she makes most of her sales."

"What's she selling?"

"She's selling cars. She is selling convertibles. She says convertibles are making a comeback and the best time to test them is at night, preferably during a full moon."

"I'll bet."

"What?"

"Forget it. I'm going with you."

"You're what?"

"I'm going with you, for the test drive. In the convertible. In the moonlight. With the floozie."

So that is how the two of us happened to drive up to the car dealer's at midnight to meet a tall blonde who was wearing a black slit skirt and a sweater that brought back memories of a young Lana Turner.

"Who's this?" she asked.

"My wife."

"You didn't tell me you were bringing someone with you," she said, in an injured, petulant voice that irritated even me.

"Oh, well, let's make the best of it," she said. "You drive, Ralphie, and you, dearie, may ride in the back seat. You'll get a better idea of the comfort of the car back there."

Then, as I settled into the driver's seat, she gave me a friendly and encouraging pat on the knee, and added, "Okay, Ralphie, let's go."

I detected something that sounded like the snarl of a wounded animal from the back seat, but decided to ignore it. Somehow, I doubted that it was going to be a night of friendly conversational discourse.

A short time later, after a run out Rothesay Avenue and back, we were driving up Garden Street when I noticed the steepness of the hill. In fact, it was so steep that the car slowed, coughed, shuddered, and came to a stop as we neared the street lights near the crest. A moment later it started to slide back. Obviously, there was something wrong.

"Put on the brake."

"What?"

"The brake," the blonde shouted. "The brake, you fool."

That, I thought, was a strange way to sell cars, calling a customer a fool. Then I realized she couldn't have been talking to me, so I looked around to see where the fool was who was supposed to put on the brake.

"The brake, the brake," she screamed.

Then, before I could do anything about the brake or anything else, she twisted and threw her long right leg across mine to put on the brake herself. Thank goodness for the split skirt, I thought, because she could never have made that manoeuvre while wearing a conventional skirt.

However, there was a slight complication. In order to reach the brake, and thereby save our lives, she was now, more or less, in what might appear to be a compromising position, straddling me and pressing against me in order to hold the brake firmly in place.

"What," said a fiercely cold and inhumane voice from the back seat, "is going on up there?"

"It's all right, dearie," said the blonde salesgirl, "I'm just showing your husband where the brake is. I didn't want us to slide back down the hill."

At this point, realizing we were in danger, I panicked. "Don't anyone move," I shouted, at the same time slipping my right arm around the blonde's waist to hold her in place, so she could keep her foot on the brake, to protect our lives.

"We've got to do something," said the blonde.

"What did you have in mind?" The voice came from the rear of the car but it was one I did not recognize. It sounded like that of the young child who was possessed in the movie *The Exorcist*.

"Well," said the blonde, "if Ralphie could use this fishing rod to take that phone off the hook and then use this pool cue to dial the police I am sure they would send someone to help."

"Say, that makes a lot of sense," I said, noticing for the first time that the young woman had a fishing rod and a pool cue, having just pulled them from the glove compartment of the car.

"Gee whiz," I remarked, "that must be an unusual glove compartment. Is it an option with the car?"

However, for some reason, the salesgirl seemed to have lost interest in telling me about the car's features and her reply was incoherent, so I turned my thoughts back to the problem at hand. Fortuitously, and as unusual as this may seem, there was an emergency telephone booth right there in the middle of the street. That's good planning by someone, I thought, as I took the fishing rod and started trying to remove the receiver from the hook.

Alas, it was not to be. Something had gone wrong in the back seat. The growling , guttural animal sounds were beginning to form a message that told me it was time to abandon the car. "I'm going to kill someone," said the voice from the back seat, though in all truth it sounded more like a voice from another world.

Luckily, at this point, I woke up.

The Old Woman Who
Kicks Footballs for Money

— — — — — — —
— — — — —
—

THEY WERE AMONG THE STRANGEST looking people I have ever seen.

There were four of them. One woman and three men.

They were old. Very old, over seventy and probably over eighty. They were huge, rough-muscled, and rough-skinned people who looked like they had spent their lives out of doors.

Only one of them spoke English. At least, only one of them was using the English language, and I didn't recognize the language the others spoke, though I thought they were Russians.

They looked like the Russians I had seen several years ago on a visit to Moscow. They were well bundled, wore heavy, ill-fitting overcoats; rough, heavy-duty scarves; and shapeless felt hats. They smelled of garlic.

They were in my office and I was nervous. My secretary, after letting them in, had left quickly, mentioning something about going to lunch. It was obvious why she was leaving the building. She didn't want to hear the gunshots or look at the blood on the carpet after my body had been removed.

Blood on the carpet? Well, I wouldn't bet against it. But whether there was blood on the carpet and a body on the way to the morgue or not, my secretary might just as well go to lunch. Not only would she not be helping me if these rough-looking customers actually got rough, she wouldn't even be speaking to me. At least not for the rest of the day—simply because I had shouted at her.

Even though she deserved it, I could see she was going into one of her sulks.

It all started out rather innocently when she came into my office and said I had some visitors.

"Who are they?" I asked.

"I don't know."

"You don't know?"

"No, they wouldn't tell me. They simply said they wanted to see the person in charge, the man who decides things."

"All right," I sighed, "show them in."

"You had better look at them first," she said.

"I had better look at them?"

"Yes."

So I peeked out the door, and then closed it quickly. "I am not the man in charge," I said.

"But you are ... you're the publisher ...."

"I am not the man in charge." I measured each word carefully before biting it off.

"But ...."

"Don't argue with me," I snapped. "I'm in charge most of the time. I'm in charge almost all of the time. I'm in charge when I say I'm in charge, but on days like this, with visitors like those, the editor is in charge. Fred Hazel is in charge. He is the one who sees visitors. He is in charge. Now, go out and tell them."

But when she opened the door they barged right in, all four of them.

The woman, who reminded me of Tugboat Annie, was carrying a football under her left arm. She was flexing the muscles of her right arm, opening and closing her fist. Ominously.

Then, honest to goodness, she started doing kneebends. The three men stood and watched her, nodding approvingly.

"She's warming up," said the one man who could speak English.

"Yes, I can see that," I said, apprehensively. "What is she warming up to do?"

"She kicks the football."

"In here?"

"No. She kicks it outdoors. She kicks it over buildings. She does it for money. She wants the newspaper to do a story."

"Yes, of course. Of course. We'll be happy to do a story. We should go right out to the news department. It sounds like a wonderful story."

"Will you take a picture, too?"

"A picture? Why, of course we'll take a picture. We'll go out to the news department and find a reporter and a photographer."

"Good," he said to me, and then he nodded to the old woman, who stopped doing the kneebends and threw off her coat. She was wearing huge black bloomers and a white T-shirt, red stockings, and white sneakers. It was a horrible sight.

"She'll leave the coat here," said the group's spokesman. It was a statement, not a request.

"Yes... why, yes, she should leave the coat here."

"She wants you to come outside and watch her."

"Outside?"

"Yes, outside."

So that is how, last week, in the middle of winter, I happened to be out in the parking lot of the newspaper with three foreign gentlemen and an old woman wearing black bloomers.

Perhaps you saw us. A lot of people did.

The spokesman spoke. "She wants to bet you she can kick the football over the building over there," he said, pointing to the old cotton mill building.

"That's impossible. Why, that would be a kick of over three hundred yards."

"She can do it. She'll bet you a hundred dollars."

"It's impossible," I began again, but I didn't like the way they were looking at me.

"Okay, okay... I don't want to bet, but I'll give her a hundred dollars if she can clear the building."

So one of the old-timers held the ball, the woman in the black bloomers did half a dozen kneebends, paced back about twenty feet, took a couple of practice kicks that would have put the Radio City Rockettes to shame, and took a wild charge at the ball—which she kicked along the ground for about ten yards. It finally slithered under a car.

"She slipped," was all the man said.

The four of them went into a huddle.

"She'll give you another chance," he said.

"Another chance? She'll give me another chance?"

"Yes, she says you can't kick the ball as far as she did."

"But it only went a few feet."

"She'll bet you a hundred dollars."

"All right." I'd had enough of this foolishness.

It was ridiculous, but I was freezing to death. I wanted to get it over with and get in out of the cold.

The old lady retrieved the ball and held it for me.

All I had to do was kick it fifteen yards. I would go for accuracy, not distance, and simply loft it over two or three lines of cars in the parking lot.

"Okay, let's get it over with."

She held it. I took a short approach run and kicked. She pulled it away. I fell flat on my back, and when I looked up there was Lucy from the *Peanuts* comic strip, laughing to kill herself.

And up there, leaning out the windows of the rear of the newspaper building were all my loyal, faithful, and loveable employees, laughing and screaming. "Way to go, Pub," they were shouting. "Way to go."

And then I woke up.

−30−

Where Is the Little Boy
with the Lunch Box?

————————
—————
—

I REMEMBER WHEN he started to grow up, when he took those first hesitant steps that one day would lead to manhood. His mother and I watched from an upstairs window on Mount Pleasant Avenue in East Saint John in the apartment where we lived over the B.O. Smiths. We watched as he strode for the first time to face the world and its challenges. A long time ago.

He carried a lunch box that reminded his mother of his grandfather, Eddie Sloat, who worked on the railroad, lived in Plaster Rock, and fished salmon on the Tobique River.

"Get out the frying pan and I'll go down to the river and get a salmon for supper," Eddie used to say. And his wife Phoebe would do just that because the salmon were there for the catching. That was before the rivers were dammed. Before progress took over, driving away or killing off the salmon.

In those days the boy with the lunch box was not yet five years old and there were tears in his mother's eyes because he was starting to grow up.

"Soon he'll be going off to college," she said, and she was told not to be so foolish. He was only a child heading off to kindergarten. His life was all ahead of him. His biggest challenge was to cross the street by himself on his way to a church basement for his kindergarten class.

And wasn't that only yesterday?

Yes, yesterday and almost a lifetime ago.

But the memories persist. There was a banana, a chocolate chip cookie, and a small thermos of milk in that lunch box. It was more than he would need for the morning break, and soon he'd be home for lunch. His life was in the future. It was the beginning of a long, long road.

There are other memories — memories that are nudged and jogged and revived by little incidents. Stuart Trueman did it the other day when he called to say he was about to leave for Florida. He wanted to tell me he had found some long-forgotten notes and he was trying to decipher them.

Those notes took him back to the days when the newspaper was in that old brick building on Canterbury Street and Stuart Trueman presided in the editor's office on the second floor. It was a long, narrow office at the head of the stairs, where he was all too easily available for those who would come to vent their anger on the newspaper and the editor. The floor was painted an unpleasant brown. It was crooked and took dips in several directions. That was why, the publisher of the day used to tell him, it would make no sense to provide him with an expensive carpet. It would only be ruined by the old flooring. His notes were about a visit to that office by one of my then young sons, Ricky or Randy.

Stu didn't recall which one, but the notes indicated the child was not far removed from the baby-talking stage. "Gurgle, gurgle," the young boy said as he waddled into the editor's office.

"Gurgle, gurgle," Stu replied. He himself was the father of two sons and long experienced in the art of conversing in baby language.

Soon they had established a form of communication.

This particular child, on that long-ago day in Stu's office, had something in his hand.

Now the notes on the conversation became clear. What the boy was saying was, "Look, Daddy gave me a nickel."

"But the poor kid," Stu told me in his recent telephone conversation, "had only a penny in his hand."

"You haven't changed much," he added.

But, of course, that wasn't true.

All that was a lifetime ago. The grandfather is gone. The salmon are gone. Kindergarten, school, universities, and graduations are fast fading into memories.

The original lunch box and others have long since been replaced by lawyers' briefcases.

She was a nice girl, Linda Murray was, so it came as no surprise when Rick called one night to say they would be married. He laughed a nervous laugh and said she had agreed it would be in the Baptist church. It was, too — in St. John the Baptist, with Father David Bona as the priest.

And now there is another telephone call in the night. It is the little boy with the lunch box, calling to say the first grandchild has arrived. Yes, everyone is fine. It is a girl. Blue eyes, he thought. Seven pounds, ten and one-half ounces. Big for a girl, he told us.

They would call her Mary Katherine. Maybe later Mary Kate. Pretty names. Great-grandmother Mary Costello would be happy. This would be another of her favourites. For her, they are all favourites.

So the little boy with the lunch box is no more. He has become a father and the wonderful and wondrous cycle of life continues. All too soon he will watch the years unfold and disappear.

A short time ago, in this corner, I wondered where the years had gone — so quickly, so irretrievably. Who had blinked those years away? It was I, of course, who had blinked.

Now I must do it again, this time to remove not time, but a tear. The years, though all too quickly gone, have been kind.

—30—

The Sudden and Miraculous
Return of My Hearing

_ _ _ _ _ _ _
_ _ _ _ _
_

I AM SURE ALL the occasional readers of this occasional column have been waiting eagerly to hear more about Mary Kate, and I'm sorry about taking so long to get back to you with this report of her progress.

You remember Mary Kate.

Mary Katherine Costello. Infant child. Daughter of Richard Bruce and Linda Murray Costello — a small, helpless bundle of beauty and energy who is just starting the wondrous journey of life. Among other things, the first grandchild.

Mary Katherine, a pretty name, I observed at the time of her birth. I also speculated that her parents would probably call her Mary Kate when she grew older. That sealed it. Ever since they have called her — Katie.

Not that it matters what they call her. She is an independent child and answers only when the spirit moves her. Most of the time she is busy strutting around her house, talking up a storm, and, literally, it seems, taking charge of everything. And why not? She is almost one and one-half years old.

However, it is not her age, but her beauty and intelligence I want to tell you about today. Mind you, to me she's just another sloppy little kid who eats her porridge with her hands instead of a spoon, but then I guess she probably has her reservations about me, too.

It is her mother and father and her grandmother (the one who hangs around my house) who have all but convinced me that this otherwise plain child is unusually beautiful and terribly talented. There is, they would have you believe, no other child like her anywhere.

Especially impressive, I am told, is her vocabulary. Why, she has a range of hundreds of words. Perhaps thousands. More extensive, I am told, than the vocabulary of many university professors.

Unfortunately, because of my advanced age and failing faculties, I am unable to understand all the words. In fact, I can hardly understand any of them.

To me, everything sounds the same.

Mind you, the child does make sounds. She rarely stops talking, if you could call it that. It is a constant yammer in her house and she is encouraged by her father and mother, not to mention two grandmothers. They listen to her, nod encouragement, and decide in their own minds, with the help of a good dose of imagination, what the child has said. Then they reply in kind. They are capable of spending hours carrying on a conversation with a seventeen-month-old child.

The other day, for instance, while the child was visiting at the home of her grandparents, she said something that sounded very much like "ba ba, da da."

Unfortunately, I didn't have the slightest idea what she was talking about, which only goes to show how bad my hearing really is.

I was told the child was asking for a banana.

"She is asking for what?" I demanded.

"She said," said her mother, "'may I have a banana, please?'" To emphasize her point the mother pointed to a plate of artificial fruit on the kitchen table.

I wasn't buying that. "What do you mean she asked for a banana, and where do you get the idea that she said please?"

"Because," said her mother, "she said it so clearly. She said, 'May I have a banana, please?'"

"That's right," said her grandmother, "can't you understand plain English, Ralph?"

At this point we were interrupted by the child. She said, "ba ba, da da."

"And that," I said, "is supposed to be, 'may I have a banana, please?'"

"No, silly," said her mother. "That time she asked for an apple."

"And did she say 'please' that time, too?"

"Of course," said her mother. "She always says please. She's very polite."

"Ba ba, da da," said the child, but by now I had decided to ask no more questions.

But the mother replied: "No, Katie, you can't have a banana because that isn't a real banana. Your Grampie doesn't buy real bananas for his only granddaughter. He just buys imitation ones to tease you. He's a bad old Grampie, isn't he, Katie?"

That was too much. Not only was the conversation idiotic, but she was attempting to turn the child against me. "Why are you talking to that child?" I demanded. "She can't understand a word you're saying," I said in exasperation.

"Of course she can understand, can't you, Katie? Say goodnight to Grampie, Katie, even if he won't buy his only grandchild a real banana."

But the child fooled her mother. Instead of saying goodnight, she said, "Ba ba, da da."

"She's back on the apples and bananas," I smirked.

"No," I was told, "what she said was 'Goodnight, Grampie.'"

The mother smiled a smile of self-satisfaction. The grandmother smiled agreement. The child smiled and drooled.

The father picked up his gifted and articulate daughter, a child who has a vocabulary of hundreds, perhaps thousands of words, and as they were about to leave she leaned over from his arms and gave me a wet kiss on the cheek — and, miraculously, my hearing suddenly returned, because this time when she said "ba ba, da da," I knew exactly what she was saying. It was in fact "Good night, Grampie."

Laura Calls the Coppers

– – – – – – –
– – – – –
–

ON REFLECTION, I'd have to say it was not a bad idea. Maybe not a great idea. Maybe not an excellent idea — but not a bad one.

What I'm talking about is Laura's reason for calling the cops.

Laura, you see, is five years old, and when she found herself all alone in that big house, well, that just didn't seem right.

There's something spooky about a large house with all those rooms and all those closets, and the beds that things can hide under, and the playroom down in the basement where it is great fun to roll on the floor and watch television. But not when you're all alone. Not when you're only five years old.

Not when you call out for your mother or your brothers or your sister. And no one answers.

That's spooky.

So Laura went to the telephone and called the police. She told the police no one was home and she thought she'd better call them because they would know what to do.

But, wait, I'm getting ahead of my story.

The reason no one was at home when Laura arrived is that the teacher at kindergarten had let the class out early. This threw things off schedule at Laura's home because the babysitter was not there when Laura arrived.

So Laura went through the house looking for someone. For anyone.

She called out for her mother, but there was no answer.

She called out for her brothers and her sister, but still there was no answer.

"I know you're here somewhere," she probably shouted. In fact, someone had to be there. Someone was always there.

But no one answered.

So she went to the phone and called the Rothesay Police. She said she wanted to report a missing child, sort of.

"Who," she was asked, "is missing."

"I am. I'm missing here in my own home. I'm all alone and I'm only five years old. I'm too young to be alone," she said for emphasis.

The police agreed, but they also figured she was making too much sense to be in any sort of trouble.

"Are you sure you're all alone?" they wanted to know.

What did they think — that she had locked the babysitter in the closet or the basement and now was reporting that she was alone? Grownups are hard to figure sometimes.

"Yes," she said, "I'm sure."

"Well, what do you want us to do?" There didn't seem to be any reason for alarm. She was calm, articulate, and in control.

"I want you to come and get me," she said.

"Why? You sound all right. Your mother should be home soon."

"Well, I'm only five years old and I think I should have police protection."

That did it.

The police had their lights flashing as they turned into the driveway to be greeted at the front door by Laura Costello, five years old, daughter of Rick and Linda Costello, soon to be the most embarrassed parents in the Town of Rothesay.

Five minutes later the babysitter arrived, right on schedule.

Still later the mother pulled in, mortified. Then, in due course, the father. What to do now?

The mother wasn't thrilled when she came home to learn she'd had a visit from the police. Nor was she enchanted with the thought of what the neighbours would be thinking if they believed she was leaving a five-year-old alone at home.

But, still, she had to admit, the child had handled it in a pretty impressive manner.

The father thought Laura should be commended, perhaps even rewarded—on the understanding that in the future she might first check with the neighbours, or call him at the office, or one of her grandmothers. Grandmothers like to get calls from their grandchildren, he told her.

As for Laura Costello, she thought she'd done the right thing. After all, that's what the police are for, isn't it—to protect five-year-old kids?

—30—

THE SPOKEN WORD

The Strange Parallel of Two Literary Lives: Senator O'Leary and Alden Nowlan

– – – – – – –
– – – – –
–

[*Editor's Note:* This is an address Ralph Costello made to the annual St. Patrick's Society dinner in Saint John.]

THIS IS ST. PATRICK'S DAY — and we are here to honour the patron saint of Ireland and to recall the sacrifices and rejoice in the deeds and the accomplishments of the Irish.

We're here to recognize the achievements and the heritage of those sons and daughters of Ireland who have contributed so much to the development, to the fabric, to the social conscience of this city, this province, and this country.

It is traditional, I know, for the speaker at this dinner to recall and revere the memory of our ancestors who made Saint John one of the most Irish and one of the proudest Irish communities in North America.

I'd like to do that tonight — but not this time by talking only about the courageous Irish immigrants, some of whom died and others who survived those savage days on Partridge Island, and not for once by talking in detail about D'Arcy McGee and his contribution to the founding of Canada, though we will honour their memories forever.

269

But tonight I want to talk, if only briefly, about some of the colourful and dynamic people—those of Irish ancestry—who have walked the streets of Saint John in our lifetime—those who helped preserve and hand on their traditions to the people of this generation and for the benefit of future generations.

I want to talk about some of these people because they remain strong in my memory and because of the lasting impact they have had and will continue to have on this city, with its proud and lively and boisterous and culturally uplifting Irish background.

I know there would be nothing original—certainly nothing original at this dinner on this night—if I were to bring back, however fleetingly, the memory of Andy Duffy, the most wonderful Irish cop of all time.

Those of you who are old enough will, of course, never forget Andy Duffy at the head of King Street. He was more Irish than Pat O'Brien, because Andy Duffy was real, he was there for all of us to see, he was there as a symbol of the police force. He wasn't an actor, he was the real-honest-to-God goods, and he was Saint John's. And would you believe he has been gone for forty-four years? Is it possible he has been gone for forty-four years? Yet his memory lives on so strongly.

And within a stone's throw of the head of King for so many years, we had what was then the most wonderful hotel in this city, and the impresario of that hotel for so long was Ned Sweeney. He was a man who could make you feel at home, really at home, whenever you were in his hotel—a man who would take care of your needs the way hotels should take care of its customers.

And if you went down Charlotte Street, not too far, in those times of Andy Duffy and in the times of Ned Sweeney, one of the then good restaurants of Saint John was run by Dan Morrisey. And turn a corner and you would be in Daley's Diner—Daley's Dog Cart—all part of Saint John.

And if Andy Duffy was the champion traffic cop of Saint John—and in many ways the champion cop of North America—there were other champions, and in King's Square we have today the monument of Charlie Gorman, the world speed-skating champion.

Let's move quickly down King Street, pausing only long enough to tip our hats to the Kennedys of Kennedy's Shoe Store and the Higginses of Higgins Haberdashery, and then along Dock Street to the corner of Dock and Union, where I'd like to take you back briefly in time to the working quarters of Saint John's first, and perhaps only, but certainly authentic leprechaun.

He had his offices, as all of you know, on the second floor of that corner building where he went through his life posing as a dentist. But he isn't a dentist, he wasn't a dentist. He is and has been and always will be a living, breathing, authentic leprechaun.

In later years we have seen Dr. Jimmy O'Brien take on more and more of the characteristics of a leprechaun. He smiles and he laughs and his devilish eyes twinkle and at any moment you might expect him to snap his fingers and disappear in a puff of smoke or whatever leprechauns disappear in.

And if you were to continue from there up Main Street, it would not be long before you would come to the business establishment of Dick Grannan — R.L. Grannan, Sir Richmond Grannan, a great Irish gentleman, servant of the people in so many ways and so many community endeavours, politician and community leader. He was a one-time city councillor and he served, if I remember correctly, on a council at about the time that a young, black-haired Paul Barry was also on council.

And if you continue to the corner of Main and Douglas Avenue, it would not be surprising if you bumped into Mike Harrigan, and if you didn't bump into him there, you would surely find him at St. Peter's ballpark or in some boxing club or at some other street corner, dodging and weaving and ducking in conversation with old-time fight promoter Jack McAllister.

Because if you talked with Jack McAllister, you'd better do a lot of dodging and weaving because McAllister had a habit of reliving all the fights he had ever seen, and he was forever demonstrating how someone was knocked to the canvas in some long-forgotten boxing match.

Mike Harrigan was as Irish as his name. He was my idea of everything a hardrock Irishman should be. Now, on days when Judge Harrigan is putting fear into the criminal element of this community, I sometimes think of tough old Mike — and I'm sure he does, too.

But, wait, that reminds me, and we should move back for a moment to the centre of the city to the courts and recall the contributions at the bar and on the bench by Ned Henneberry, the silver-haired magistrate, the colourful orator, the one-time president of this society — and we should think for a moment about the lasting contribution that his life had on this community.

In fact, we should remember and honour the memory of so many Irish immigrants who came to Saint John — certainly those who fled the famine of 1847 and others who came and found their first jobs, established their roots, and raised their families in Saint John while working in the ironworks, at the nailworks, in the breweries, on the waterfront, at the cotton mill.

It was at the cotton mill that my grandfather worked as a foreman; in fact, his whole family worked there with him, because in those days if you were a foreman and if, not incidentally, you were Irish, you sure found jobs for your own.

It was a mixed blessing — because many of the Costellos and many others died young deaths, victims of the working conditions in the mills of those days — and victims all too often of the ravages of tuberculosis.

But some of those hardy Irish immigrants survived, some escaped from the mills and went on to make their own personal contributions to the development of this city and the preservation of the culture and the heritage of Ireland that had been brought to these shores by their ancestors.

But this is not to be a night of sad memories, so while we're still in the East End let's think of names such as Binks O'Leary. Binks O'Leary: what a wonderful lyrical Irish name that was.

And Binks, like Andy Duffy, was real. He was a baseball player, he was handsome and graceful, and he played with teams that came out of the East End and they were wonderful baseball players. Paul McGrattan was another of that era, and there were many, many more.

Danny Britt would remember those times and those colourful baseball players and so would many of you.

Because this is our background; this is where so many of us came from.

And now, quickly over to Fairville, where you'd find the O'Tooles and the Maloneys and the Driscolls and Arthur Carton and, yes, that famous hockey line, the one-time kid line, Garey, Butler, and O'Toole. And if you lived in Saint John in those times, you would have known Fred Hazel — the real Fred Hazel — the one who knew something about music, not the other Fred Hazel, who himself, come to think of it, is looking more and more like a leprechaun as time goes on.

Gentlemen, I said earlier it was not my intention tonight to speak at length on the privation, the suffering, and the courage of those Irish immigrants who spent their first days and weeks and months on Canadian soil on bleak and forbidding, grave-cluttered Partridge Island.

But I do want to speak about courage and willpower, ambition, accomplishments — I want to tell you about those of Irish ancestry of humble beginnings who have risen to be leaders in their fields, and I want to suggest that we honour their memories and emulate their accomplishments.

In doing so, I want to use the words of an earlier speaker who, in answering the question, who are the Irish? said that, in part at least, they were of royal origin but humble birth.

I want to recall the careers of two men of humble birth who touched our lives in Saint John, two men who stand out as shining examples of how the thirst for knowledge and the determination to overcome the crushing handicaps of their beginnings won for them places of prominence and respect as leaders in their fields in Canada.

I will take just a moment to tell you about the first man, using his own words:

> I was born in Percé, on the Gaspé, on February 19, 1888. My father was born there, too, his father having fled the Irish potato famine in 1847 and settled on a scrub farm area, making a life from the land and sea. I grew up in a settlement called Irishtown Road, where every cabin had three pictures — the Pope, Parnell, and John L. Sullivan. I left school aged eleven, but lived there until I was fifteen.
>
> When I was a young boy, a bell summoned the workers at dawn to trawl out fish to be dried on the flakes. They were given an hour for lunch and they worked on until dusk, and often were summoned out again until midnight. They received, as I remember, about seventy-five cents a day.
>
> But the people of Gaspé also had small farms, farms which did not bring them wealth but which gave them security and a sense of manhood and dignity. They grew their own grain. They cut

it with a sickle, and they threshed it with a flail. I myself engaged in these activities. They took that grain to the local miller and brought back feed and flour for their livestock and for themselves.

They killed their cattle and took the hides to the local tannery and brought back leather, and they had that leather made into boots and shoes by the local shoemaker. They lived by the light of candles made by themselves. They sheared their sheep. They put the wool on the snowy slopes to bleach. They brought it into the homes and carded it. They spun it into yarn on old spinning wheels, and then took it to the looms, which were in most of the homes, and wove it into good homespun.

While I say this was not affluence, it was not extreme poverty, and it had the great merit of preserving the manliness, the dignity, and the courage of the individual.

Now you ask me what education I had. Very little, unfortunately. But I think the present approach is wrong. Education is not something to make a man a lawyer, a doctor, an engineer, or priest. It is something to make him a man. The true education is not to give a man a standard of living, but a standard of life. I speak with some feeling on this.

I never went to high school, but God was good to me in that I knew an old bishop in Gaspé, Bishop Bosse. His sister lived on an adjoining farm to ours, so he sent me his books. He was a remarkable man. He sent me biography, history, poetry, and novels. He once even sent me the sermons of that famous Baptist divine, de Witt Chalmers.

I never had a grammar lesson, but poetry gave me a sense of the beauty and economy of words. We had lots of Irish newspapers, from Dublin and the *Freeman's Journal*, from New York the *Irish World*, from Minneapolis the *Irish Standard*. We knew more about British politics than Canadian.

When I read these books, I read them by candlelight with candles made in our own home. What did they do for me, those books? They made me think that I must explore that outer world.

I got to know about that world which is far, far beyond the Gaspé coast. I worked in a lumber mill at the age of twelve. I went to sea at the age of fifteen and remained three or four years.

I came ashore in Saint John, New Brunswick, and worked in the Saint John ironworks, in the Pinder nailworks, and in a brewery. I worked in a hardware shop. I went up to Richibucto, a little windswept village on the Northumberland Strait, and worked in a store. I got a job as a reporter in 1909 on the *Saint John Standard*, which I am sure was a bad thing for journalism, but at least it saved my spirit and my soul. I have never thought of the state looking after me, never. I never thought of it, I expect, until I guiltily entered this chamber in the Senate.

That man, as many of you would recognize — and certainly as Premier Hatfield and Senator Dan Riley would know — was Michael Grattan O'Leary, a leading Canadian journalist, editor, orator, and a distinguished senator. He was a long-time president and editor of the *Ottawa Journal*.

He went from the scrub settlement of Irishtown Road on the Gaspé to become one of our most respected and distinguished Canadians.

But that, you might be tempted to say, was another time, another era — why, he was born in 1888, another century. It is no longer possible, you might say, in our society to overcome the handicaps he faced in early life.

Let me, therefore, tell you briefly about another outstanding Canadian who started his life in much the same circumstances.

He was born, not in the nineteenth century, but as recently as 1933 in a Nova Scotia village so wretchedly poor that he called it Desolation Creek. In that Depression winter of 1933, his father worked as a lumberman for a dollar a day. His mother was fifteen, and she left when he was a few years old. His house had no electricity, only the most primitive of heating and certainly no indoor plumbing.

He quit school in grade 5, got a job in the woods and later as a watchman at a sawmill, and this gave him a chance to spend most of his nights reading.

He discovered a library in Windsor, thirty-two kilometres away, and walked or hitchhiked there every Saturday for armloads of books.

Later he was to work at the *Hartland Observer* and the *Telegraph-Journal*. He was to win recognition and countless awards as one of Canada's most gifted writers of prose and poetry.

Tragically, he was to die, far too young, at the age of fifty.

He was Alden Nowlan—and his life should serve as a challenge and a inspiration to all of us.

What did these two unusual and outstanding Canadians have in common? Many things.

Both were Irish, but they were more than Irish by birth—they were Irish to the core, proud of their humble beginnings, proud of their homeland, proud of their ancestors and their heritage.

When Alden Nowlan was buried, the pipers played jigs and reels, the pallbearers toasted him at graveside with Irish whiskey, and his family and friends shovelled the dirt over his coffin as gravediggers stood aside and watched in mild bewilderment.

Both left school in grade 5, both worked in lumber mills at the age of twelve—but neither ever stopped his education.

They devoured books and they devoured knowledge—and then they dispersed that knowledge wisely, widely, and well.

They loved the language and they became self-made masters of it.

In Saint John they brushed our lives, all too briefly, and we are better for it.

Each in his own way was a great Canadian—we should remember them and we should honour their memory.

And while the world has changed and continues to change, and while the technical and professional demands of society are much different and much greater, we should remind present and future generations of the opportunities that still exist for those of humble birth who persevere at all costs in the search for knowledge, in the quest for wider horizons, in the determination to meet and overcome adversity—for that, too, in its own way is the story and the history of the Irish of Saint John and the Irish of the world.

—30—

Fred Hazel's Book Launch,
March 14, 1996

— — — — — — —
— — — — —
—

ORIGINALLY, it had been my intention to open these remarks by welcoming everyone to what I understood was to be the launching of Fred Hazel's book — *Get Yerself a Shin O' Heat* — or, if you prefer, *Fred Hazel and the Irish Connection*.

That is how the program was explained to me several weeks ago when, somehow — obviously in a moment of delusion — I got the impression that I would be the speaker of the evening.

I also was left with the impression that this would be a small, informal gathering at which I would be expected to say something nice about the book, something flattering about Fred — and then everyone would drink a glass and one-half of wine (by Danny Britt's calculations), buy a book, and go home.

A glass and one-half of wine?

Well, that, as you know, was later cut to half a glass, and Danny assigned his wife Olga to guard the bottles and pour. With an eyedropper.

When I looked at what I had been offered — with the wine brimming up to a point where it almost covered the entire bottom of the glass, I told Olga, facetiously, I thought, that she was pouring with too heavy a hand.

She replied, straight faced, that Danny had already warned her about that.

Incidentally, from the very beginning, from the time when I was first asked to speak, I had lived with the illusion that this would be the very first introduction of the book — but that was before Gerry Childs got his hands on a copy and somehow managed to say everything in his review that I had intended to say tonight. Even — as I recall it — quoting something very profound that I had once written about Fred, which I would otherwise have used tonight on the assumption that everyone would have forgotten it by now. But now — if I were to repeat what I wrote originally, you would think that I was stealing from Gerry what he had borrowed from me.

Still, this is a wonderful book, and there is much left for me to talk about — or at least there was until Fred started his morning sessions on the CBC, determined, it appears, to read us every bloody word from his own book.

All of which left me wondering what I would say tonight — and who would be left to hear it.

And then it came to me.

No one had touched on the index.

Not a single word had been written in praise of the index.

Gerry had missed it. The CBC had overlooked it. And I was reasonably sure — reasonably sure but not certain — that Fred would not read the index, even if it did include a scintillating list of names of people and places covering eight full fascinating, tantalizing pages at the very back of the book.

This constituted about five per cent of the book — unexplored and unreviewed... an absolute goldmine of information.

So that is what I will talk about tonight.

Go to the letter H and up pops Bob and Tom Higgins... and someone named Adolf Hitler.

You'll find Jean Chrétien and Elsie Wayne between the covers....

Skip over to R and you'll meet a fiery politician named Louis Robichaud, and if you take direction and go back to pages 134–135 there's more than a hint of a night of revelry involving young reporter Fred Hazel and the then-newcomer to the New Brunswick political scene.

You'll also learn that Fred believed in being prepared for almost anything in those days. So, in anticipation of an evening when he would entertain the Liberal leader, he went to the liquor store to stock up on a supply of white lightning. Did he buy enough? Did he buy too much? For that answer you will have to read the book — but I'll give you this much of a hint: his guest was Louie Robichaud.

Finally, if you stick with the index to the very end — to the final Z — you will meet Gianni Zwaetta.

Gianni Zwaetta?

Sure, someone Fred met in an Irish pub — in Italy.

An Irish pub in Italy? Well, you must remember you're travelling with Fred Hazel.

But enough about the index. After all, I don't want to give away all of Fred's best stuff.

I should introduce Fred and say a few words about the book.

Which I now will do.

I have known Fred for almost half a century and now — through this book and Fred's unusual talent as a writer — I have come to know him as a very young boy living in a modest home in Fairville and dreaming those impossible dreams that could never come true. But then, in so many ways, they did materialize, and Fred not only lived out his dreams but now he takes readers along on a remarkable journey all over the world. This lifetime journey brings Fred — and his readers — back inevitably, happily, and lovingly to within a stone's throw of where it all began, to the community that, I am sure, Fred still thinks of as Fairville.

I first met Fred in the late 1940s when he came to work at the newspaper. He was nineteen or twenty, I suppose, but as Gerry Childs wrote so accurately, looked more like a kid of fourteen.

This book will actually take you back in time until you find yourself standing beside a small boy who is looking fearfully at the shadows at the end of a long, dark hallway in the Hazel home.

Fred is not yet six years of age — and he is afraid. There is nothing particularly unusual about this — except that, in this case, in this book, in this story, you will find yourself there in that long hallway with young Fred Hazel, sensing the worry of a little boy, sharing his emotions and his fears, as he is taunted by his older brother, Joe.

That is part of the magic of this book — part of the writing skill that will take you back in time not only in Fred's life, but in your own as well.

Those of you who read this book — and I expect all of you will — will be there for Fred's first kiss, or at the very least the first kiss that meant something very special to him. Yet, almost miraculously, you will not feel that you are there as an intruder. It is yet another tribute to his skill as a writer.

I should tell you that *Shin O' Heat* is not an autobiography — or at least I don't think it was intended to be an autobiography — but you will travel with Fred on a wonderful journey from that dark Fairville hallway until, sixty years later, you find yourself in the company of a bunch of old men. Because we are old now, even Fred, and there is no escaping it.

So you will end up with these men sixty-five to seventy years of age — all of them St. Vincent's High School graduates at their fiftieth anniversary reunion, all of them trying to recapture their long lost youth, all of them shouting out a Hikety, Chike, a Hikety Chike, and so on … their old high school yell.

And you'll think it has been quite a trip and I'm glad Fred invited us along…

But, wait. Am I telling you too much? Am I giving away the plot?

I don't think so.

You see, I can say as much as I like about this trip — but only Fred can take you with him — as he does so well, so convincingly, so intimately.

−30−

A Tribute to Cliff Warner, May 24, 2000

––––––––
–––––
–

FOR SOME REASON—and I don't quite know what it was—but when I was considering how I would open this tribute to Cliff Warner, I found myself thinking about Patty Berg.

She was an outstanding golfer back in the 1930s and long after that.

Back in those days in the 1930s, young Patty Berg possessed that very special beauty of the girl next door, or the girl you wished were living next door. She had a wonderful smile. She had a face full of beautiful freckles. She sparkled with radiance and freshness.

Many years later I would meet Patty Berg—now a charming, older woman who somehow had retained all the freshness and sparkle of that young girl of yesteryear. This time she was speaking at an international meeting of golf officials.

She started her talk by saying, "I'm going to have to tell you a story or two to get warmed up."

She then told the story of the time she was playing in a tournament with an inexperienced caddie. After a few holes she was on a fairway about 190 yards from the green. And she said to the caddie, "Do you think I can get home with a two iron?" The caddie replied, "I don't know . . . where do you live?" She knew then it was going to be a long day on the links.

Well, for Cliff and for me, it has already been a very long day on the course...a long trip that goes back sixty years and more.

And, Cliff—I must say I had to smile when I read Wayne Chapman's announcement in the newspaper about this award.

Cliff Warner, that announcement said, would receive the Red Triangle Award for exemplifying the mission and the philosophy of the Y movement.

In short, Cliff Warner was to be honoured by the Y—by the YM-YWCA.

Well, how times change.

Why, sixty years ago, those of us, or at least some of us, at the YMCA hated everything there was to hate about you and your gang at the YMCI, which was later to become the CYO.

Come to think of it, if it had been suggested sixty years ago that you be honoured by the YMCA, it is likely someone would have gone over and burned down the old YMCI building.

Of course, that would never happen today.

And hate is probably too strong a word for the rivalry, but there certainly was no love lost between the YMCA and the YMCI in those days now so long ago.

That rivalry was very real. Among other things, it had something to do with basketball.

The fact is, and if I have to be honest, Cliff—you guys were getting too good at the game, with players like Ray Lawlor, the Kirk Brothers, the Conlon Brothers, Charlie Whelly, Murray Champ Bowes, and several others.

And a little later—and you were part of this, Cliff—there were players like Ted Owens, Bill Ritchie, Ralph Lawless, Paul Byrner, Harold Horgan, and Father John Mooney, who dished out so much punishment under the basket that he had to go into the priesthood and spend the next fifty years of his life saying Hail Marys or whatever it is you people say when you have sinned.

Then there was that little guy named Esmonde Barry. He could play basketball all right, but he always thought his way was the only way.

I remember when we at the YMCA believed all league games should be played at our gym because, we said, it was better than the YMCI gym—which, of course, was true. Es Barry, however, objected, and said if he didn't get his way he'd organize a protest group and write letters to the newspaper and everything.

I remember once when we were arguing the merits of playing all games at the YMCA, he said, "I suppose you'd like to have only one hospital in the city, too." And then he added, "Well, it ain't going to happen."

I don't know what that was all about, but that's how I remember the conversation of sixty years ago.

Cliff, even then, sixty or more years ago when our paths first crossed, you were already setting your life's pattern — you played some basketball, but you were more active as a team manager, someone a bit behind the scenes, a worker . . . someone who got things done.

I believe that is how most of us think of Cliff. Someone who gets things done. While others of us are out front taking the bows, Cliff is that silent Rock of Gibraltar who gets on with the job — the job of making this a better place, especially for those in need, but also a better community for all of us.

There are, of course, those among us who think of Cliff Warner as a quiet, pensive, thoughtful, and even shy person.

But there is another side to Cliff Warner.

Most of us have seen it — but perhaps not often enough.

Cliff has a great self-deprecating sense of humour. He enjoys life. He has a wonderful smile and an engaging laugh. He has gone through life as a happy warrior.

At home, I am told, he was — and continues to be — a terrible tease . . . and with five sisters I expect he had plenty of practice.

But it wasn't only his sisters that Cliff teased and tormented.

One of his favourite targets was his brother John, who later became a prominent lawyer in Fredericton.

I knew John years ago. We called him Jack in those days, and he was typical of this unusual family. Back then — a long time ago — Jack was a school teacher. In his spare time he articled at the local law office and worked several nights a week at the newspaper.

Perhaps because of his newspaper background he always wanted to listen to the nightly news at ten o'clock on radio and probably later on television.

Cliff — the tease and the tormentor — knew this, and whenever Jack was trying to listen to the news at home, Cliff would attempt to engage him in conversation.

Jack, in turn, would ignore him.

But Cliff, not to be denied, would simply raise his voice above that of the announcer and at some crucial point in the newscast would speak even louder and ask Jack for his opinion on some totally unrelated and irrelevant subject.

Finally, when Jack would blow up and tell Cliff to get lost, Cliff would put on his innocent act.

"What?...what?...what did I do?", he would whine in mock dismay "...I didn't know you were trying to listen to the radio."

And then he'd smile that little boy smile, that cat-that-ate-the-canary smile...because he'd succeeded in getting the needle in once again.

However, and despite these idiosyncrasies, I believe it is fair to say that most of us would think of Cliff as being more of an introvert than an extrovert, but we should also remember that he has been known to do many things on the public stage in Saint John, even, I have been reminded, appearing in a fashion show.

Which might seem a little out of character until you hear the story of the other time he got dressed up in a velvet vest and purple pantaloons and all the other regalia to take part in a Loyalist Day celebration. I don't really know that the pantaloons were purple, but it makes the story all the more outrageous.

But just imagine the shock his brother Don, the priest, experienced when he came upon Cliff about to leave the house.

"Dear Mother of God," the priest said (that's the way priests talk, you know)—"Dear Mother of God, Cliff, you're not going out like that."

Cliff said he was, and to add insult to injury—or maybe it was injury to insult—he asked his brother, the priest, if he would hook up the back of his costume.

His brother, the priest, did so, reluctantly.

Cliff went out, probably to chaperon or go dancing with Elsie Wayne or Shirley McAlary at some Loyalist Day event—and his brother went wherever it is priests go to pray for the redemption and salvation of the soul of his dear, demented brother.

Why does Cliff do these things that on the surface seem so out of character? He does these things, he takes on these roles—because he is asked, because it is yet another event for a worthy cause, because it is good for the community.

Because Cliff is Cliff, and we would have him no other way.

For as long as any of us can remember, whenever this community has needed someone with bulldog determination ... whenever there has been a need for commitment and leadership, we in this community have turned to Cliff Warner.

We'd identify the problem, and then in effect we'd say, Sic 'em, Cliff.

And he'd be there to answer the call whether it was the United Way, the Victorian Order of Nurses, Family Services, the Knights of Columbus, the St. Rose Community Housing program, the board of the Lord Beaverbrook Rink, the Bi-Capitol Committee—and a dozen and more other volunteer and charitable organizations.

In fact, his record of service is absolutely staggering.

I, like many of you, have watched him in action and I, like many of you, have had the pleasure of working with him.

Cliff and I were on the board of the Riverside Country Club about thirty-five years ago when we were building what was then the new clubhouse. Cliff had been president of the club and by then I was president, and he was keeping an eye on the finances.

As the new club neared completion, we realized we were going to be $17,000 over budget. I, as president, took full presidential responsibility—and blamed everything on Cliff, the financial man.

So I asked him what he was going to do.

He told me not to worry ... he'd think of something.

The next day the old club burned to the ground.

By coincidence, insurance on the old club by this time had been reduced to $20,000, so this gave us a margin of $3,000, and we also saved the cost of demolishing the old clubhouse.

We never did find out how that fire started.

And for thirty-five years I have kept—and will continue to keep—my promise never to refer to Cliff Warner as Cliff the Torch.

Incidentally—and I know this has no bearing on anything related to our ceremonies tonight or that long-ago fire at the Riverside Country Club—but it has occurred to me that we recently lost to fire that old YMCI-CYO building at the corner of Cliff and Waterloo Streets.

There was a report—and I just mention this in passing—that, right after the start of the fire, an elderly gentleman was seen fleeing the scene. He was described as being rather stocky, perhaps in his fifties, sixties, seventies, or maybe even his eighties, with a high forehead (whatever that means).

I gather the building was well insured, as it was also said that while all of this was going on there was the sound of violin music emanating from what used to be known as the Bishop's Palace.

Well, I guess we can discount both of those reports because I expect the last thing you'd hear from the Bishop's Palace would be fiddle music. Bishop Bray would never permit it.

I presume Bishop Bray is still the guy in charge over there.

Now, back to reality.

It was not long after our experience on the board at Riverside that Cliff and I were back together in the United Way. I was general chairman of the campaign, and Cliff—who later would be campaign chairman and president—was chairman of the budget and admission committee. Among other responsibilities, Cliff would review, and adjust, the budgets of all member agencies—and he did this for years. He was very meticulous, very fair, and the United Way had some extremely good years in serving the community while budgets were under his personal scrutiny.

Cliff is a living example of someone who has achieved personal success, respect, and admiration . . . and perhaps most important of all, he has shown us over and over again the personal joy that is to be found in giving something back to the community.

We are here tonight to honour Cliff Warner, but in a very real sense I look on it as a tribute to the entire Warner family and what that family and individual members were able to achieve.

This was a family of the Depression, but it also was a family of outstanding spirit and accomplishment.

There were five beautiful sisters—and that is how they were known. Cliff also had four brothers, and the entire family, brothers and sisters alike, would achieve success. They were teachers, lawyers, executives, a doctor, a priest, an RCMP officer—and, of course, Cliff himself.

I knew Cliff's father, who, I suspect, brought some of that bulldog determination to the family...and then there was the mother, who, I am told, was a wonderful person who instilled pride and spirit and compassion in the entire family.

I only wish, as I am sure Cliff does, that more of them were still with us, and able to be here tonight to witness and applaud this well-deserved recognition for Cliff.

Cliff and I have lived long enough to see Saint John grow into a community that is more tolerant, more caring, more ecumenical. School rivalries and other rivalries still exist — and I hope they will continue, because they foster competition and young people learn to rise to the challenge of competition, and usually are better for it.

But in Saint John the bitterness and the distrust and, yes, even the hate of another era are largely behind us.

And Cliff Warner is one of those in this community who created a new bridge of understanding and friendship — for those who once were on different sides of the fence of prejudice and intolerance — a fence that Cliff Warner has helped dismantle by his example, by his personal service to the community and his compassion for others.

Saint John is a much better place for all of us because of the Cliff Warners of this world.

Personally, after watching this remarkable career of a remarkable man over a sixty-year period, I am extremely pleased to be here tonight to see him recognized and honoured.

So, congratulations to you, Cliff — and I commend and congratulate the YM-YWCA for making such a wise and popular selection.

−30−

Remarks at the Memorial Service for Jack Brayley, Wallace, N.S., August 15, 1991

-

WHEN ZEVERSA AND SALLY (BRAYLEY) first asked me to speak at this memorial service, I thought of myself as an unlikely choice. The reasons were many—among them the fact that I had not spent much time in church in my adult life.

I also had a vivid memory of the last time I had accepted an invitation to speak in a church—to address a meeting of the Saint John Ministerial Association on the subject of the church in China following a visit to that godless society. On that occasion, and just as I was about to enter the church, the skies opened up, thunder roared, and lightening flashed across the heavens.

Was this, I wondered, some form of ecclesiastical fanfare provided for speakers, or possibly some Higher Power welcoming home a prodigal son? Or perhaps, more ominously, an expression of heavenly displeasure that someone of questionable religious status was about to enter those sacred chambers?

Well, despite my misgivings, Zeversa was very persuasive, telling me that she and Jack had always enjoyed listening to me speak—and, in truth, I am, of course, very pleased to be here to honour Jack's memory and to pay tribute to one of the giants of Maritime journalism.

I will always remember Jack as I am sure he would want to be remembered—as a working journalist. As a reporter. As a reporter's reporter—as the mentor of many journalists who learned at his knee and under his lash that they'd better get it first, they'd better get it right, and that once it was on the Canadian Press wire it was the bible and it had better be the bible's truth.

I should tell you, right at the beginning, that I will not attempt to recount the whole story of Jack Brayley's life in journalism—or the many other things he accomplished in such a busy and productive life. That would be impossible.

But I will tell a story or two about Jack—stories which I hope will remind us of the qualities and the stature of this unusual man—this high school dropout who lived life so warmly, so fully, so productively, and with such great zest—this reporter, editor, and broadcaster who became something of a giant of journalism in this section of Canada.

One of the strongest and most lasting memories many of us have is that of Jack Brayley on the night of a provincial election. That was the night CP would move into the newsroom of, say, the *Telegraph-Journal* in Saint John back in the days when the newspapers would become the real election-night headquarters in the province. It was the same, I understand, when Jack and his staffers descended on other newsrooms for other elections around the Atlantic provinces. Jack, on those occasions, was the master of a quiet, orderly, efficient news operation. It was an experience that everyone should see at least once in a lifetime, as Jack's calm and soothing voice would waft serenely across the newsroom, just barely audible over the crashing keys of those old iron typewriters of another era.

If I remember correctly, he was known as Whispering Jack Brayley on those occasions—and if you believe that, I will have a sale of Brooklyn Bridge share certificates available at the end of this service, and I will assume that you never had the pleasure of seeing or hearing Jack Brayley and his CP team in full and furious flight on an election night back in the 1940s, '50s, '60s, and probably on into the '70s.

It was, believe me, a sight to behold.

This was long before the days when computers would predict election results almost within minutes of the early returns. But we were not without our computers—Jack Brayley was the human computer. The human dynamo, a bull of the woods, and, yes, a bull in a china shop, a rampaging bull shouting directions, conceding or awarding seats—and when he said he was giving the Conservatives the seat in Queens South, he meant just that. The computer—Jack Brayley—had spoken and out it went on the CP wire.

It was a sight to behold — an experience never to be forgotten. It was Jack Brayley at centre stage in the life he lived and the life he loved. It was old-time journalism. It was Jack Brayley in his own element, in the centre of a loud, pulsating, decision-making newsroom on election night — and it was Jack Brayley in charge, himself something of a raging dynamo of energy and commitment.

There was another Jack Brayley.

There was the Jack Brayley who was first, foremost, and always a news reporter.

Jack Brayley, Reporter.

He was a reporter who believed in getting it right. He felt an obligation to CP, to the member newspapers, and to the readers of newspapers. He believed they were entitled to the full story, the intimate details. A story that answered the key questions. A story that left the reader fulfilled and informed.

I was reminded of Jack's own talent in painting the complete picture when I had an opportunity to read his book, yet to be published, that he so appropriately titled "Man Bites Dog." That book is a treasure of the exciting life that he and Zeversa lived together for more than half a century — and it is also a treasure and a memory of the famous and near-famous who were part of the life of Jack Brayley, Reporter, for that same half-century.

Now, briefly and quickly, I would like to remember another Jack Brayley — Jack Brayley, Old Man. This was not a good time in Jack's life. It was not a good time for Zeversa and the Brayley family.

But even during the dark days of Jack's illness, his terrible frustrations, and the sad and trying days for Zeversa as she watched this giant of another time grow old and feeble — even during these difficult times there were moments, however brief, of brightness and laughter and, yes, brief times of small accomplishment and large happiness.

Jack Brayley did not go down easily. He did not go down without a fight. Let me recall a couple of incidents.

It is something more than a year ago that Jack and a grandson arrived at my office for a visit. This was Old Jack Brayley. An old man who could just shuffle a few inches at a time. He hated it. Being dependent on others bothered him terribly. He was frustrated, embarrassed. After our chat I walked him to the parking lot, and as we shuffled along, I said, "Jack, you've slowed down a bit, but I'd still put my money on you in a race with Stu Trueman."

It was a moment of magic. It struck a responsive chord.

His eyes brightened, the famous Brayley smile appeared—and he said, with more strength than anything else he'd said that day, "You would? You really would? You think I could still outwalk Stu?"

"Jack," I said, "it would be no contest."

"Well," he said, "at least that's something." He laughed at the thought of it and I believe he actually speeded up—because he couldn't wait to get back to the car to tell Zeversa. That was Jack Brayley, Old Man—an old man but still game, still competitive.

A year later Stu had had an operation on his knee and Jack's health had deteriorated. Both were using walkers. Then one day I was talking to Jack on the phone and he asked about Stu. I told him Stu had taken a couple of falls in his home.

"Has he got wheels on his walker?" Jack wanted to know.

"No," I said, "I don't believe he has."

"Well, tell the damn fool to get some wheels on his walker before he falls and kills himself."

Now, one final story.

As Jack grew weaker he became more and more anxious about his book. He wanted to see it published, yet his health did not permit him to deal with it, to handle revisions, to negotiate with publishers. Again, this was a time of great frustration.

This was understandable. "Man Bites Dog" is as unusual as its title. It is unusual because Jack was determined to write about everything his youth, his mother and father, Zeversa, his family, and that daring young couple, Jack and Zeversa, who went off to London on a grand adventure in the 1930s.

He wrote about wars, about world figures, presidents and royalty, about conservation, camping, about national parks, neighbourly news, about CP—and all the personalities he had rubbed shoulders with in about as exciting a life as anyone would ever want to live.

But, as it turned out, it was not a book that was ready for publication. However, it contained wonderful stories, and I was able to arrange for a series of articles to appear in the *Telegraph-Journal*—in the newspaper where it all had started more than sixty years ago. It was a lively series, well illustrated and strongly displayed. And Jack's byline was back in print—back, again, in the *Telegraph-Journal*.

Soon, I had a telephone call from Jack Brayley, Reporter. The voice was weak, faltering — and Jack remained maddeningly frustrated because he couldn't spit out the words the way he wanted to. But it was the voice of appreciation. A different voice. Now, when it cracked or faltered it was because of emotion brought on by happiness.

I had more calls from Jack. More happy calls because old friends wrote to him to say they had read and enjoyed his articles in the *Telegraph-Journal*.

Jack's voice, I felt, became stronger. It seemed younger. His terrible frustration, for a brief moment in time, was gone. Then the series was about to end, and I had another call from Jack. He wondered if the newspaper would consider another article or two. There were some important things that hadn't been recorded.

There was nothing demanding about the request. He was simply hopeful that the newspaper might see fit to wind up the series the way it should be wound up. I said I thought something might be possible.

Two days later I had a letter from Jack. It was crisp. It was sharp. It was to the point. It was the kind of a message news editors write when they want to be sure that things are handled right. It was the kind of a memo I had written myself thousands of times.

Let me read you Jack's last letter to me.

Dear Ralph:

You were again kind enough to offer to add a couple more chapters of my memoirs to round out and make them more or less complete. So, I thought it might be helpful if I suggested what may be used:

The Suez Crisis
The Korean War
The Spanish Civil War
Cyprus
Royal tours and Montgomery

My coverage of world fliers
A brief reference to my advice on good journalism.

For your consideration,
Jack.

It was all quite proper. It all made sense—but this was not a message from a frustrated old man. This was a memo from Jack Brayley, Reporter; Jack Brayley, Editor; Jack Brayley, CP Bureau Chief.

So, for a brief moment in time, for a few days, as his byline appeared for one final time and while his stories graced the news columns of his old newspaper—Jack Brayley lived once again the heady experience of a reporter, an editor—a newsman.

It was a short and, I think, happy interlude. It was not something that could last—but for that brief whisper in time Jack Brayley returned to the love and the sunshine of his life, and for him—and certainly for me—nothing could have been more rewarding or more gratifying.

Soon, however, Jack's health became more of a problem and it was obvious that, in a sense, he had had his Last Hurrah.

But Jack was to have one more triumph.

Because—and I say this to his old friend, to one of the co-discoverers of New Brunswick's Magnetic Hill—to Stu Trueman, I say, Jack Brayley has beaten you and all the rest of us old reporters to the barn once again.

He's out there—up there somewhere—smiling down on us because he knows something we don't know. He's scooped us once again, one last time.

And I'll bet he's found an old newsroom where CP teletypes are clicking and clacking, where telephones are ringing, and those iron typewriters are making the beautiful music that only an old reporter can appreciate.

I expect he's up there with Gil Purcell and John Dauphinee, with Dougie Amaron and Charlie Bruce, with Don Covey and Dal Warrington, and people like John Mosher, Ross Munro, and Stu Keate, and a lot of other giants of his time.

And you can bet Jack Brayley's smiling down on all us today—as only Jack can smile.